The solitary flute sounds
A tune beyond the clouds
Apart from those who know its voice
Who else recognizes it?

BOOKS BY J. C. CLEARY

The Blue Cliff Record (three volumes, with Thomas Cleary), 1977.

Swampland Flowers, 1977.

Zen Lore from the Source Mirror, 1979.

Zen Dawn, 1986.

A Buddha from Korea, 1988.

Zibo: The Last Great Zen Master of China, 1989.*

Recorded Sayings of Linji, forthcoming.

Wumen's Barrier, forthcoming.

Worldly Wisdom: Confucian Teachings from the Ming Dynasty, 1991.

Pure Land, Pure Mind, forthcoming, 1991.

Meditating With Koans, forthcoming.†

* Published by Asian Humanities Press.
† Forthcoming from Asian Humanities Press.

A Tune Beyond the Clouds
Zen Teachings From Old China

Translated and Edited by
J. C. Cleary

Asian Humanities Press
Berkeley, California

ASIAN HUMANITIES PRESS

Asian Humanities Press offers to the specialist and the general reader alike the best in new translations of major works and significant original contributions to enhance our understanding of Asian religions, cultures and thought.

ISBN 0-89581-901-5

Library of Congress Catalog Card Number 91-70001

Printed in the United States of America

Contents

Preface

In presenting this collection of Zen teachings I have departed from my past practice of leaving the translation to speak for itself with only minimal explanatory notes.

The teachings translated here come from a period in history when Zen discourse had reached its maximum point of intricacy. The beauty of the imagery is immediately apparent, but the religious message being expressed would probably remain mysterious to anyone without a long immersion in Zen literature.

Consequently, with material like this, my task as a translator would not be complete without supplying some pointers to help decipher the metaphoric codes being used. Obviously the brief explanations I provide are only hints as to where the meaning lies. To penetrate to the depths of the Zen masters' multiple layers of meaning, it will still require the readers' own personal effort.

I have added a brief introduction to the Zen analysis of the human mind and the Buddha Mind, to supply a general frame of reference into which particular Zen teachings fit.

Also included is an account of Zen history, and the history of China in the period in which the Zen masters whose words are translated here lived. This may serve to dispel the fantasy that Old Asia was a serene land of spirituality where wisdom came easy. A much deeper and truer appreciation of the great Zen masters is obtained by realizing that they were flesh-and-blood people living in a world full of ignorance, hatred and strife, and not the inhabitants of a fairy-tale "mystic East".

Why do we continue to provide translations of classic Zen lore? So that modern people interested in Zen can encounter the authentic style of the Zen school, and to provide a reliable standard of comparison for judging the words and deeds of contemporaries who advertize themselves with the word "Zen".

A Word on the Transliteration

Chinese names are transliterated into Roman letters in this book using the standard Pinyin system.

To get a rough idea of the actual pronunciation of the Chinese names, the reader might want to bear the following points in mind:

Most consonants in Pinyin have sounds similar to their values in English, with the following notable exceptions:

X represents a sound similar to English SH

Q represents a sound similar to English CH

C represents a sound similar to English TS

ZH represents a sound similar to English J

The use of vowels in Pinyin is more complex.

A usually as in father. After Y or I, A sounds like E in get.

E after Y or I sounds like E in get. In other positions, sounds something like U in nut.

I usually sounds like I in machine. After CH, SH, ZH, and R, the letter I represents a sound something like the UR in hurt, but pronounced with the tongue higher in the mouth.

O usually sounds like AW in awful. In the combination ONG the O sounds like OO in foot. OU sounds like O in note.

U usually sounds like the OO in food. After Q, X, and J, U sounds like U-umlaut in German, or the French U in deja vu.

Introduction

I. "A Tune Beyond the Clouds"

This work focuses on the teachings of an outstanding Zen master of old China, a man we will call Stone River. Shiqi Xinyue, whose name can be translated as "Mind-Moon of Stone River," lived in South China in the thirteenth century, during the waning years of the Song dynasty. Stone River was one of the acknowledged leaders of the Chinese Zen community in his own time, though little is recorded of his personal life. He served as abbot of various major Zen temples, and was honored by the imperial authorities as an eminent holy man.

The thirteenth century was a turbulent time for China. The country was invaded and conquered in stages by the armies of the Mongol confederation, and subjected to the capricious rule of the conquerors. Along with the new rulers came new religious and cultural interests, along with a new pattern of politics and government, and more intense exploitation of the common people. Stone River lived in the eye of this storm.

One aim of this book is to let readers reflect on the relationship between the world-transcending Buddha Dharma, and the worldly history of the people among whom the Dharma is being taught. Stone River's recorded sayings contain occasional comments that reflect a clear awareness of the historical moment in which he was working, and the tasks facing Buddhist teachers at that point in the history of Buddhism in China. Naturally his principal focus was on how to keep the Buddhist teaching itself alive. Like all true Buddhist teachers, he worked to keep the teaching of enlightenment from being swallowed up by ritual, routine, emotionalism, and misguided ambitions. Amidst the deepening gloom and increasing pressures of the contemporary secular world, Stone River could best fulfill his vows of compassion by keeping open the door to genuine liberation for whoever had the right motivation to enter.

So borrowing a phrase from one of Stone River's verses, I have entitled this collection of Zen words "A Tune Beyond the Clouds" in order to symbolize the timeless aspect of the Zen teaching, beyond the shifting clouds of delusion and worldly disorder.

II. A Slice of Zen History

1. Buddhism in China

By the time of the Mongol conquest, Buddhism had already been in China for a thousand years. Over five hundred years had passed since the first great flowering of the Zen school in the eighth century.

The full story of Buddhist history is not easy to trace. Buddhism existed on many levels simultaneously in medieval China. It was an institutional presence, with temples and monasteries a common sight in the cities and towns, and shrines and retreats scattered across the countryside. Buddhist monks and nuns with their distinctive costumes were a recognized part of the population. The public festivals and ceremonies put on by the monks and nuns of the major temples punctuated the yearly calendar. Sacred mountains located in various parts of China were great centers of pilgrimages by the faithful.

Buddhism was also a complex of beliefs, practices, rituals, and legends. Stories from the Buddhist scriptures had passed into popular culture, and become familiar parts of the storytellers' repertoire. People could see a variety of buddhas and bodhisattvas depicted in statuary and paintings and woodblock prints. Manuscript and printed editions of the Buddhist scriptures were on display in temples and monasteries, and were included in the book collections of wealthy laymen. On many ceremonial occasions, the scriptures were chanted aloud by monks and nuns, so that even the illiterate had an opportunity to hear their teachings. People turned to Buddhist monks and nuns to preside at funerals, to pray for the sick, and officiate at services to comfort the souls of the dead.

Many people in old China accepted a popularized version of the Buddhist teaching of karmic reward and punishment. In Chinese popular Buddhism, the principle of karmic retribution, of reward and punishment according to one's deeds, was fused with the family-centered concerns typical of Chinese culture. The average Chinese Buddhist believed that bad deeds sooner or later would bring punishment, not only to evildoer himself, but also to his kinfolk and descendants. Similarly, the merit gained by good deeds could be transferred to improve the karmic prospects of one's family members.

In their attempts to accumulate merit on behalf of themselves and their kinfolk, people prayed to buddha-images, recited sutras, made offerings at temples of food and money and flowers and incense, and hired monks and nuns to chant scriptures and perform ceremonies. True believers tried to adhere to Buddhist precepts against taking life, lying, stealing, adultery and intoxication. The faithful often made vows, pledging to keep the precepts and perform specific good works. As a symbol of their commitment to live Buddhist lives, they formally "took refuge" with the Three Jewels of Buddhism, the Buddha (the Enlightened One), the Dharma (the Teaching of Enlightenment), and the Sangha (the Community of monks and nuns).

Though monks and nuns played a key role in many ritual contexts, Buddhism in China was also a religion of the laity. There were many lay Buddhists who tried to the best of their ability to serve Buddha by pious acts like giving alms to the needy, or donating funds to have scriptures copied, images cast, and temples refurbished and decorated. According to their means, they gave material support to Buddhist institutions and clergy. Lay believers strove to observe the ethical code of Buddhism, to familiarize themselves with Buddhist scriptures, and to serve Buddhist teachers. They prayed to buddhas and bodhisattvas for protection and aid.

Lay Buddhists often formed groups that met together regularly for religious purposes: to chant scriptures, listen to Buddhist lessons, or to burn incense to offer homage to the Buddha. Such groups frequently had their own meeting halls and treasuries, supported by the members' donations, and they would offer material aid to members in need. Laypeople's associations had their own rules and regulations for members, and sometimes members had to confess their sins publicly before the group. Some groups were led by monks or nuns; some by especially devout laypeople or by leaders who had inherited their positions.

Pure Land Buddhism attracted many believers. The teachers who first propagated the Pure Land teaching in the sixth and seventh centuries pointed out that for many people the quest for enlightenment as outlined in the Buddhist scriptures, through a long rigorous process of self-discipline, was too demanding. They observed that ordinary people were generally too mired in bad karma to have any hope of salvation through their own efforts. The Pure Land teaching offered the prospect of salvation through faith in Amitabha Buddha, the Buddha of Infinite Life. All who invoke Amitabha Buddha with sincere faith, regardless of their sins, are promised rebirth in the Pure Land through the power of Amitabha. The Pure Land is a paradise where people can continue to strive for ultimate enlightenment free from the sufferings and obstacles of this world.

Down through the history of Chinese Buddhism, there were many groups of believers who met regularly to chant the name of Amitabha. Pure Land groups multiplied in times of trouble, when the secular world offered little hope, and the bonds of evil karma seemed to grow heavier. Not only laypeople, but many Buddhist monks and nuns followed Pure Land practices. Invoking the name of Amitabha could be done individually or in groups, silently or aloud. Besides chanting the name of Amitabha, believers usually took vows to dedicate themselves to attaining rebirth in the Pure Land Land. Pure Land literature is full of edifying death-scenes: after long years of invoking Amitabha, the dying man or woman reports to those gathered at the deathbed visions of the Pure Land opening up to welcome him or her into paradise.

Not all Buddhists always recognized the special claims of the Buddhist clergy. In Chinese history there were various revival move-ments among the Buddhist laity that criticized the Buddhist clerical establishment for moral laxity and worldliness. These "protestants" argued that people in lay life could best pursue the goals of the religion by rejecting the corrupt clergy and dedicating themselves to strict observance of the basic tenents of Buddhist morality.

There was a millenarian current within Chinese Buddhism that gave the secular authorities no end of political trouble down through the history of the Chinese Empire. The millenarian Buddhists believed in the coming of Maitreya, the Future Buddha spoken of in various scriptures. Once Maitreya was born on earth, the millenarians believed, the corrupt, unjust social order of the present would be overthrown, and a new age of peace, prosperity, and justice would come into being.

Not surprisingly, the imperial authorities viewed such beliefs as subversive heresies, and the millenarian versions of Buddhism were generally outlawed. But despite government attempts to eradicate them, in many regions of China Buddhist millenarian communities persisted through the generations as clandestine organizations, with their own leaders, sacred prophetic texts, and social networks. Many many times in Chinese history, when the millenarians judged that Maitreya was about to come or had already been born among them, they would launch uprisings aimed at overthrowing the imperial authorities and cleansing the world of its accumulated wrongs. Under most circumstances, the government was strong enough to drown these rebellions in blood, and the millenarians were scattered and driven underground again.

2. The Zen Schools

The Zen schools arose in China after Buddhism had become thoroughly assimilated into Chinese life. The basic scriptures and philosophical treatises of Indian Buddhism had been skillfully translated into Chinese. Buddhist stories and images had become well known among the Chinese people. Buddhist philosophy had been mastered and synthesized by Chinese Buddhist savants. Popular forms of Buddhism had developed into a whole spectrum of ritual and faith found among the Chinese people. The Buddhist teaching on karmic reward and punishment had been widely accepted at all levels of the social hierarchy. Buddhism had become institutionalized, and had attracted lavish patronage from the high and mighty, as well as the material support of ordinary Chinese. Buddhist temples and Buddhist clergy were everywhere. Buddhist rites had been incorporated into the life-cycle, and Buddhist festivals were part of the yearly calendar.

The founders of Zen observed the paradoxical result of this widespread "acceptance" of Buddhism: the forms of the Buddhist Teaching were being venerated and worshipped, but the essential message was not being put into practice. The Zen teachers stressed that the Buddhist scriptures were not meant to be idolized as sacred texts, but were intended to be utilized practical guides. They taught that Buddha himself was not to be seen as a remote, super-human figure, but as a model to be emulated in everyday affairs. To them enlightenment was not a distant goal obtainable only after countless eons of effort, but something to be achieved by dedicated efforts in the present life.

With this insistence that the Buddhist Teaching be brought to life in the here and now, and the personal example of its teachers, the Zen school gave new impetus to Chinese Buddhism (and to Buddhism throughout East Asia). From the eighth century onward, the Zen teaching was established throughout China (and spread to Vietnam and Korea and eventually Japan). Seekers flocked to the teaching centers where the Zen masters were at work. Records of the sayings and doings of Zen teachers became a new genre of Buddhist literature. By the tenth century, Zen had become the intellectually predominant form of Buddhism in East Asia. Zen influence was felt not only within Buddhist thought and practice itself, but also in the art, literature, and philosophy of the wider culture.

3. Zen Influences

From the fifth century well into the seventeenth century, Buddhism and ideas deriving from Buddhist philosophy occupied a considerable place in Chinese high culture, the intellectual culture of the educated elite.

In the main, of course, upper class people shared in the beliefs and practices typical of popular Buddhism. They were just as eager as their unlettered compatriots to accumulate merit and expiate bad karma by paying for rituals and making offerings. Their greater wealth enabled some of them to patronize Buddhist institutions on a grand scale, donating lands and buildings, paying for the upkeep of monks and nuns, and contributing great sums of money to pay for images, ritual finery, copies of scriptures. Rich and poor alike tended to adopt a manipulative attitude toward ritual, attributing a magical efficacy to the forms of worship, and imagining they could make religious obser-vances serve worldly aims.

But beyond this broadly shared popular Buddhism, more subtle Buddhist ideas and concepts, particularly in the form given them by the Zen schools, also penetrated into the most refined heights of Chinese culture.

The great revival of Confucian philosophy that occured under the Song dynasty during the eleventh century owed an obvious debt to Buddhist influences. As the Zen masters had done within the Chinese Buddhist tradition, the great figures of Song Confucianism claimed that it was not enough merely to revere the classical teachings and acquire a superificial knowledge of them by rote learning. The real goal, they insisted, was to put the classic teachings into practice in everyday life, to make a conscientious effort to live up to the example of the sages.

Many Song period Confucians openly embraced Buddhist ideas and pointed out parallels between Buddhism and the teachings of the Confucian sages. Even those Confucians who emphatically rejected Buddhism had to admit the great attraction Zen Buddhist ideas exercised on the contemporary Confucian intelligentsia. From the Song dynasty onward, many Confucian gentlemen took up forms of meditation very much like certain practices of the Zen school.

The Buddhist influence also made itself felt on Taoism, the age-old indigenous Chinese tradition of mystical cultivation and practical arts. Taoist texts were gathered together into collections modeled on the Buddhist canon. The styles of meditation and discourse characteristic of the Zen school reappeared in Taoist guise. The masters of the new schools of Taoism that were formed in the Song period knew the Zen school well, just as Zen masters knew and quoted from Taoist sources. Given the intrinsic harmony of outlook between mystics of the two traditions, it is not surprising that Buddhist and Taoist teachers recognized a common ground between them. The verbal teachings of the adepts of the two traditions appear in many instances to be the same message expressed in two different codes.

Meanwhile, Zen Buddhism in particular was having a great influence on Chinese literature and art. The startling originality and richness of metaphor typical of Zen literature fascinated many Chinese writers and poets. Chinese philosophical discourse, even that of the opponents of Zen, had to answer to Zen perspectives. Chinese painting too received fresh insiration from Zen-influenced artists, who communicated a unique viewpoint showing a seamless harmony of abstract pattern and concrete realism.

4. The Process of Buddhist History

How did it happen that Buddhist influences came to permeate so many aspects of Chinese culture, from popular belief to high culture?

The self-contained character of Chinese culture can be exaggerated, but down through history it is true that the Chinese people and particularly the Chinese elite have cherished a strong sense of the superiority of their own values and customs over those of foreigners. Not until the advent of the modern political and scientific ideas forced on the attention of China by the superior military power of the West, did a complex of ideas originating outside China have such a pervasive impact on Chinese culture as Buddhism. And Buddhism, needless to say, was not spread by gunboats.

Surely it was a long process, a matter of centuries from the time when Buddhism first arrived in China as a religion of foreigners, through the period of translation and gradual acculturation, through the rise of specifically Chinese formulations of Buddhism. By the time of Shiqi and Daian, where we pick up the story in the present book, a whole range of Buddhist forms and ideas had become familiar, long-accepted parts of the Chinese religious and cultural landscape. How did this remarkable development take place?

The view of this process from within the Buddhist tradition is reflected in Buddhist histories and in theoretical discussions of the method of teaching.

Buddhist sources suggest that the key role in the transmission of Buddhism at all levels was played by the enlightened adepts, who were the real conduits of the world-transcending Dharma into the world of conventional social reality. Sometimes the adepts worked in obscurity, sometimes they were known locally as teachers, sometimes they functioned as famous public figures. Sometimes they did not appear to the world as "religious" figures at all, but were active in other arenas, such as community organizing, cultural endeavors, and even politics. By no means did reputation in the world and real religious attainment always go together.

But whatever the extent of their public role and contemporary renown, it was the teachers of genuine insight, the independent masters of the Dharma, whose work was most crucial to the spread of the teaching. Why? They were the experts in skill in means, who devised and pro-pagated conceptual systems and forms of practice and carried on the vital work of adapting the timeless teaching to the needs of specific times and places. They were the ones who communicated the Dharma at the intimate person-to-person level, seeking out people whose sincerity and capacity made them suitable candidates for learning the Dharma. They were the originators of the patterns that gradually diffused outward, interacting with and being influenced by Chinese culture and society.

It was this process of interaction between the teaching designs of the adepts and the surrounding environment of pre-existing Chinese cultural norms and practices that gave Buddhism in China the shapes it gradually took on. Considered as individual cases, the impact of the work of the Buddhist adepts might seem minimal, barely deflecting the vast momentum of Chinese life and culture. Buddhist teachings were swallowed up by a society set in its ways, that interpreted (or misinter-preted) them in a manner congenial to its own predelictions. But overall, the fact remains that through the cumulative affect of the work of many teachers, Buddhist ideas and practices were planted at all levels of Chinese society.

Buddhist sources give careful attention to the process of interaction between the designs of the enlightening teachings of the adepts and the habit-patterns and mentalities of the people of the world. The Buddhist masters pointed out that practices and ideas originally designed and propated as skillful means to promote enlightened awareness were regularly "captured" by the mundane world, and engulfed by the human preference for ideologies and simple routines. The instrumental value of teachings would be ignored, and they would be taken as something to believe in and venerate, as emotional props for a way of life.

In this fashion, teaching forms would gradually become fragmented, distorted, fossilized, worshipped as ends instead of means, vitiated of their enlightening force. This is why Buddhist history was marked by successive waves of enlightened adepts who came forth to combat these all-too-human tendencies. The teachers of each new cycle would work to redirect attention away from outward forms back to ultimate intent. Their task was to revivify, rework, and refresh traditional forms, and to create new forms and institutions. Along the way they also explicitly pointed out the working of this whole process of deterioration and renewal.

5. Zen in the time of "Stone River"

By the thirteenth century, as the Song dynasty headed for its final downfall, Zen Buddhism in China appeared outwardly to be flourishing. The major Zen temples were among the largest, wealthiest, most prestigious Buddhist institutions in the country, and were included in the official system of government-recognized temples. The imperial government regularly bestowed honors on the leading Zen teachers. Song poetry, painting, and philosophy all showed traces of the Zen outlook. Even the opponents of Zen in China had to admit that many of the best minds among the intellectual elite were attracted to Zen models.

Within the Zen communities, the picture was mixed. The respectability and public acceptance of the Zen schools attracted more interested people, but it also gave more motive for would-be imitators. The institutionalization of Zen gave it a recognized presence in society, but also provided more room for those who sought worldly profit through a religious career, who served the "wheel of food" rather than the "wheel of the Dharma". The intellectual prestige of Zen discourse helped communicate the Zen message more widely, but it also tempted shallow self-promoters to give themselves airs of wisdom by trying to counterfeit Zen-style sayings.

In the Song period Zen literature flourished as never before. The tangible legacy of centuries of Zen teaching had been gathered together and set forth in published collections. Old manuals of monastic discipline were published, and new ones composed. The classic teaching stories were assembled along with commentaries in prose and verse. The recorded sayings of the great masters of the past were published and circulated widely in the Zen centers. Casebooks were put together to chronicle the esoteric lessons of more contemporary Zen masters. Collections of correspondence between Zen teachers and literati in lay life were published. Zen men wrote philosophical works to bring out explicitly the underlying complementarity of Zen and the Buddhism of the scriptures, and of Zen and Pure Land Buddhism.

This proliferation of Zen literature offered great opportunities for spreading the teaching, but it also presented certain dangers. Literati were attracted to the surface beauty and conceptual subtlety of Zen sayings, but sometimes forgot the deeper purpose for which Zen sayings were designed. The intellectual prestige and the aesthetic appeal of Zen literature prompted some writers to attempt to copy the style of Zen discourse, even though they lacked the insight that lay behind it. As commentary was added upon commentary, Zen writings reached a level of extreme intricacy and sometimes became excessively in-grown and self-referential. Only the initiated would be in a position to discern the real message conveyed in such a complex code, and to distinguish the genuine article from imitations.

By reading Zen literature people could acquire an intellectual knowledge of Zen theory, but without the properly directed personal effort necessary to put the theory into practice, they would not realize the enlightening effect. After a superficial study of the great compendia of "public cases" people sometimes imagined that they "knew the answers" to the Zen koans, without having done the meditation work that was needed to benefit from the koans. A second-hand knowledge of Zen gained from Zen writings might give people the illusion of possessing esoteric knowledge, but in real-life situations they would be just as helpless, just as much as the mercy of feelings and events, as the untutored, ordinary worldlings.

"Lip-service Zen" was the term applied by the real Zen masters when they warned against these tendencies. They continued to remind people that Zen sayings were meant as practical tools to refine the mind, not as intellectual playthings or emotional/aesthetic stimulants. From the Song period onward, Zen teachers combated the rising tide of lip-service Zen in many ways. They called it by name and frequently denounced its errors. Leading teachers repeatedly emphasizing the link between Zen and the Buddhism of the sutras, to make it clear that Zen sayings were not fancy verbal concoctions, but practical pointers on the map of the greater reality illustrated in the scriptures. They said that to attempt to study Zen without a thorough knowledge of scriptural Buddhism was like trying to run before learning how to crawl. They used familiar Zen sayings in novel ways, to challenge the complacency of those who held to pat interpretations and looked no further. And they continued to describe the indescribable Dharma in new ways that showed the multiple depths of meaning and the creativity and freshness of metaphor that no mere imitators could match. By such means the Zen adepts continued to respond to the imperative of their own tradition of communicating world-transcending truth.

6. The Barbarian Conquests of China

Meanwhile, in the twelfth and thirteenth centuries, the secular society of medieval China was plunged into a period of military and political emergencies.

Song China was culturally vibrant and economically strong, but proved to be militarily weak, even though its military establishment was very large, and extremely expensive to maintain. How could this be?

For one thing, the Song Empire was ruled by a civilian bureaucracy that distrusted the military and kept it in check by a system of divided powers and close controls. Every effort was made to insure that military commanders could develop no power base of troops loyal to them personally. When units of the main army were deployed in frontier defense, civilian commissioners were appointed to oversee (and second guess) the field generals, who were given command only on a temporary ad hoc basis. Local military garrisons were deliberately weakened and the most effective military forces were centralized in the capital area army groups, where they could be more effectively supervised by the civilian authorities.

If we try to account for the military debacle of Song China from the point of view of classical Chinese political theory, the fundamental cause of Song military weakness was the lack of solidarity in Song society. The Chinese classics teach that no state can be strong in the absence of strong bonds of mutual loyalty and trust between the rulers and the ruled, between the upper classes and the bulk of the population.

But this was far from true in Song times. Wealth and political power was distributed very unevenly in Song society. Educational opportunity was mostly confined to the upper class. There was a relatively small class of big landowners living in comfort who monopolized political power and community leadership. Meanwhile many smallholders and tenant farmers who barely eked out a living rendered heavy taxes and labor services to the state.

The first great shock to this fragile structure came in 1126 and 1127, when the main Song armies suffered crushing defeat at the hands of the Jurchen. The Jurchen were the ruling tribe of a kingdom to the northeast of China. Their realm had an ethnically mixed population perhaps a twentieth as numerous as China's, but with a vigorous warrior aristocracy. Unlike the despised conscripts of the Song armies, the Jurchen soldiers had a personal stake in the spoils of victory, and bonds of personal loyalty with their commanders. In the Jurchen invasion, the Song emperor and his court were taken prisoner, and the Song regime lost control of the northern plains of China. With the main Chinese armies smashed and the political elite captured or put to flight, popular resistance to the foreign conquerors was localized and sporadic, and ineffectual.

The Jurchen and their vassals ruled North China as a caste of military conquerors, confiscating lands and making serfs of the peasants who worked them. Wherever possible they coopted influential Chinese landowners and used them as officials of their new regime. Many upper class Chinese from the north fled south. In the first few years after the conquest of the north, the Jurchen armies raided and plundered major Chinese cities below the Yangzi River, but gradually the remnants of the Song regime reestablished their authority with a new capital south of the Yangzi River.

China was divided in two: the Jurchen controlled the North and called their regime the Jin (meaning "Golden") dynasty, the while the Song dynasty continued in the South and is usually known to history as the Southern Song. Between the two states, running across the Huai River valley of central China, was a shifting zone of border raids and skirmishes.

Gradually, the Jurchen ruling class in North China came to adopt Chinese culture. They set up a Chinese-style bureaucracy to oversee their non-Jurchen subjects, and used an examination system to recruit Chinese to be officials. Military commands, the key positions of power, continued to be the monopoly of Jurchen nobles. Skilled craftsmen, artisans and entertainers, and many wealthy educated Chinese as well, were brought to the Jin capital to serve the new masters. By the middle of the twelfth century the Jin rulers were using Chinese titles of nobility and Chinese court etiquette. The economy slowly recovered from the turmoil of the conquest period, and the giant urban centers bequeathed by Song period regained some of their former glory. The Jin rulers became patrons of Buddhism and Taoism and even Confucianism. Buddhist and Taoist teachers of note were active among the Jurchen elite.

The Southern Song regime ruled over the richer, more populous half of China. South China was a densely populated, economically developed region, with a network of cities and market towns linked by rivers and canals. In many areas, the agricultural economy was commercialized, with farmers specializing in growing cash crops for the market. Textiles and porcelains and all manner of handicrafts were produced in abundance in the workshops of the cities and towns. The great prosperity of domestic and overseas trade enabled the Southern Song government to rely on commercial taxes for a large share of its revenues. The great landowners and great merchants, in league with the imperial bureaucrats, formed an entrenched political elite.

The economic and cultural center of South China was the region known as Jiangnan ("South of the River", roughly equivalent to modern Zhejiang and Jiangxi provinces). The cities of Jiangnan were where the promising scholars, writers, artists and philosophers came to make their careers. Jiangnan was also the center of gravity of institutional Buddhism, a territory dotted with numerous grand temples, richly endowed with lands and bound laborers. Shiqi, whose Dharma words are translated below, was a native of the Jiangnan region.

In the generation after the Jin conquest of North China, a kind of military equilibrium developed between the Jin and the Southern Song, owing to the internal limitations felt by the two sides. The Jin rulers initially had their hands full knitting together their local commanders into a centralized regime and recruiting capable collaborators among their Chinese subjects. The newly constituted Southern Song court was wary of letting its generals achieve too much independent power, and reined in those who advocated a war of reconquest in the North.

Another round of warfare occured in the 1160's. The Jin attempts to invade the South were thwarted, and the Song counter-offensives north of the Yangzi River were likewise beaten back. Both sides were feeling internal political strains, and were content to let a generation pass without major military efforts. On the Song side, the central government was in no position to attempt to divert control of people and economic resources away from the landed magnates, in order to mobilize the resources of society for military adventures. Meanwhile, within the Jin regime, there were fierce power struggles among the courtiers and aristocrats, complete with land confiscations and assassinations. The Jin leaders became alarmed by the growing sini-fication of the Jurchen people, and tried in vain to reverse the consequent decline of the old-time martial virtues. With the leadership of both sides conscious of their weaknesses, and dedicated to a cautious policy, the result was a military stalemate.

But a new political factor was about to come onto the scene. In the early years of the thirteenth century, a new power arose in the grasslands north of China: the Mongol confederation. Uniting the steppe tribes under his rule in 1206, Chinghis Khan built up a powerful army by organizing the tribes' manpower into units under the command of his own loyal lieutenants and kinsmen. The Mongols would soon destroy the Jin dynasty and eventually conquer the Southern Song as well.

The Mongol pressure began to increase on the Jin just as a new round of warfare broke out between the Jin and Song in the early 1200's. Bribery of opponents and intrigue at home played as much of a role as the actual fighting in the inconclusive conflict between the Jin and Song. But while the Jin and Southern Song forces were preoccupied with each other, the Mongol war machine was acquiring unstoppable momentum. By 1214 the Jin position north of the Yellow River had disintegrated under Mongol pressure, and the Jin elite relocated south of the river and made the walled metropolis Kaifeng their new capital. The Mongols occupied northeastern China. In 1218 the Jin desperately sued for peace, but the Mongols spurned their offer. Only the diversion of Mongol forces to wide-ranging campaigns in Central Asia postponed the final downfall of the Jin. In the 1230's the Mongols completed the destruction of the Jin dynasty, and occupied all of North China.

The Mongol conquest of North China was extremely destructive. Those who refused to surrender and dared to resist were punished by ruthless slaughter. Unaware at first of the "civilized" forms of exploi-tation through taxation and rent, the Mongols were guided by the belief that conquest gave them total power over the conquered. The Mongol armies spread out across North China like giant raiding parties, subjecting the local people to extortionate demands for supplies, and freely taking captives away with them. They felt no compunction about levelling towns and villages, driving the peasantry off the land, or taking so much that their victims were left nothing to survive on. The Chinese cities, which were centers of upper-class life where wealth and luxurious goods were concentrated, became prizes to be taken and plundered.

Certainly institutionalized Buddhism did not escape unscathed from this prolonged ordeal for society at large. Major temples were also concentrations of wealth and presented obvious targets for conquerors. When big temples were looted and burned, not only were holy images and ritual finery and valuable scriptures destroyed. The congregations of monks and nuns who dwelled in these temples were killed, captured, or driven off: the survivors fled among the people.

South China was spared for another generation from the ravages of the Mongols. This was not due to the military prowess of the Southern Song regime, but to the fact that the Mongols were busy with further conquests in Korea, Central Asia, Russia, Iran, and the Middle East, and the Mongol leaders were preoccupied with their own internal power struggles.

This delay in the Mongol invasion of the South had positive consequences for South China's cities and for its Buddhist establishment. The Mongol conquerors had a generation in North China to learn the advantages of regularized exploitation over devastating plunder. They gradually acquired a knowledge of Chinese ways of government and taxation. In time the Mongols came to feel for the sanctity of Buddhism and Taoism, and to invoke them for supernatural protection and aid. Accordingly, when the Mongol conquest of the Southern Song came in 1279, South China was spared much of the generalized wanton destruction that the northern part of the country had had to endure forty years earlier. Chinghis Khan's grandson Qubilai Khan (reigned 1260-1294), who presided over the conquest of the South, was interested in ruling more in the style of an Emperor of China than as a barbarian chieftain.

The Yuan dynasty (as the Mongol regime in East Asia styled itself) came to adopt more and more a Chinese-style facade, but the key positions of power remained in the hands of the Mongol aristocracy. In fact the dynasty never became a highly centralized regime like the Song. The central government directly ruled only the provinces in North China around the capital, while relatively autonomous regional military administrations controlled the outlying areas.

Qubilai did what he could to give the Yuan regime a centralized government. He dispatched trusted members of the Imperial Guard to act as overseers to supervise the collection of supplies and conscription of manpower in the provinces. He tried to bring some central direction to the Mongol armies, which had remained relatively autonomous forces under the command of their own leaders. A multi-ethnic bureaucracy, including Central Asian Muslims and Jurchen and Khitan nobles from the Northeast, as well as Chinese who had worked for the Jin, functioned under the supervision of the Mongol overlords. The population was registered by occupational status and ethnic background, and head taxes, land taxes, and labor services were assigned accordingly. The Mongol nobles were granted lands as fiefs with their inhabitants as slaves to work them.

The Mongol domination opened up China to diverse new influences, and brought to the fore new men with new tastes. When it came to acting as patrons of culture and religion, the new masters displayed an eclectic bent. The new elite favored new styles of painting and literature, so that Yuan period Chinese high culture became quite different from the high culture of the Song dynasty. The Mongol nobility patronized not only Taoism and Chinese Buddhism, but also Tibetan-style Tantric Buddhism, with the result that Tantric temples and Tibetan Buddhist lamas become established in the major Chinese cities, and Tantric styles of art and liturgy found their way into Chinese Buddhist ritual.

How does the story end? The Mongols ruled China well into the fourteenth century, until their regime was overthrown by a series of uprisings led by Chinese millenarian Buddhist rebels, the followers of the White Lotus Religion.

These millenarian Buddhists believed that the coming of the Future Buddha Maitreya would bring a new era of justice and prosperity to the world. Millenarian communities had a long history of clandestine existence in China prior to the Mongol period, but in the tumultuous and oppressive conditions of Mongol domination they grew as never before. With their own economic resources and social networks, and their own ideology and special sense of destiny, the White Lotus communities provided an organized alternative to the existing society and its heartless demands. The White Lotus belief was that the Unborn Mother, the creatress of the world, would soon send a King of Light, or Maitreya Buddha himself, to overthrow the corrupt social order and its tyrannical rulers, and usher in a new era of peace and plenty. In the middle of the fourteenth century, many White Lotus groups decided that the coming of the King of Light was at hand, and they launched the armed struggle that eventually drove the Mongols out of China.

7. The Worldly and the World-Transcending

As we can see from the preceding historical sketch, the Chinese world at the time of the Zen Master of Stone River was a turbulent place, wracked by social strife and foreign invasions. Severe blows were dealt to institutional Buddhism by waves of conquest and warfare.

The question is: what impact did all this turmoil have on Buddhism itself, on the Buddha Dharma, the teaching of enlightenment? What is the relation between the history of Buddhism as part of the social and cultural order, and the history of Buddhism as a tradition of world-transcending wisdom?

Obviously, in the right hands, social prestige and the availability of material resources could serve to further Buddhist aims. To give charity, care for the aged and infirm, feed the hungry, give shelter to travellers, provide support for widows and orphans: all these worthy purposes could be carried out only by those with access to goods and money. Buddhist institutions could and did use the income from their properties and the donations they collected for such charitable activities. The ritual practices and cycle of festivals by which elementary Buddhist teachings were etched in the minds of ordinary people also called for expenditures of goods and money. The social respectability of Buddhist institutions could be utilized to attract people's attention to the teaching itself. Widespread social acceptance helped shield Buddhism from attempts of the secular authorities to interfere with it.

Nevertheless, it would be a mistake simply to equate the material wealth and social prestige of Buddhist institutions with the flourishing of the Dharma itself. Buddhist history is full of counterexamples to this facile assumption. There were times and places where Buddhist institutions presented all the outward signs of prosperity, while the Teaching itself declined into rote formalism. At other times, enlightened teachers carried out their functions with far-reaching effectiveness without the benefit of splendid buildings or wealthy patrons. The lesson of Buddhist history is that there was no simple correlation between the prosperity and social standing of Buddhist institutions in a given time and place, and the real quality of the Teaching there.

We should remember that the teachings of the Buddhist adepts repeatedly warned of the dangers of worldly motivations corrupting the pursuit of religious goals. According to the adepts, the most dangerous enemies of Buddhism were not its overt opponents, but rather monks and nuns with worldly aims. Buddhism was brought low by monks and nuns who were ambitious for fame, power and personal profit, whose main interest lay in eating well, pursuing sexual pleasures, living in comfortable quarters, and dressing in fine garments. The Teaching was perverted by monks and nuns who tailored their message to cater to the whims of wealthy donors and political patrons, or to play on the hopes and fears of the credulous. The greater the wealth of Buddhist institutions, and the higher their social standing, the greater the attraction for those with worldly motivations to seek a career as a monk or nun.

Another worldly factor with an impact on the Buddhist Teaching was the degree of religious and social freedom permitted by the political authorities in any given time and place. This issue merits attention not only in the context of China in the tumultuous historical period spanned by Shiqi in the late Song to Daian in the early Ming, but as a general question in Buddhist history.

In medieval China there was no institution corresponding to the Church in Christian Europe, politically entrenched, possessed of great wealth and centralized organization, and constantly using its pervasive influence in attempts to enforce a religious orthodoxy on the population. Throughout most of Chinese history, there was no religious institution claiming a monopoly on truth, and enforcing its role as the sole mediator between God and Man.

In that sense, there was considerably more religious freedom in China than in Christian Europe: people were free to believe what they wanted and worship as they pleased, provided that they offered obeisance to the imperial authorities and presented no political challenge. Only the millenarian traditions, which explicitly condemned the status quo and prophesied its overthrow, were generally outlawed and persecuted.

Most of the time, individual Chinese were under no compulsion to adhere to a set of rigidly defined, officially prescribed dogmas. There was no political or social pressure compelling them to pay tithes to any particular religious organization. As long as their outward behavior conformed to the required norms of social and political deference to the secular authorities, people in China were free to follow an eclectic mix of Confucian, Taoist, Buddhist, and local cults.

In their religious beliefs and observances, some Chinese gave more emphasis to purely Buddhist, or purely Confucian, or purely Taoist forms; some pursued the religious activities of the cults of local deities. But there were many people in Old China who passed easily and unself-consciously back and forth from Buddhist to Taoist to Confucian ceremonies, and their beliefs were a blend of the teachings of all three traditions. At various times, according to the tastes of the monarch and the grandees, the imperial state itself offered patronage to the notable representatives and institutions and ceremonies of all three religions. Even the local deities of the folk religion would often be coopted into the imperial pantheon, once their worship had become widespread enough.

There were a few episodes of religious persecution in Chinese history, but these were spasmodic purges aimed at institutions, more than at the believers themselves, and were generally short-lived and quickly undone. In the main, the limitations on religious freedom in Old China derived from the demands of the tightly knit social structure itself. The principal issue was to what extent people could be allowed to opt out of their social obligations in order to follow religious pursuits.

This issue was articulated in the perennial concerns of Confucian critics of Buddhism. In their view, the Buddhist clergy represented an economic drain on society: every monk was one less man to farm, pay taxes, and render labor services; every nun was one less women to spin and weave and rear children. These critics argued that the wealth lavished on Buddhist temples could be better applied to the expenses of the state. They complained that by entering the Buddhist clergy, men and women were abandoning their filial obligations to support their parents and help maintain the social position of their families.

The imperial authorities were quite aware of the fiscal issue presented by the proliferation of Buddhist monks and nuns. Both the Song and Ming dynasties at times tried to impose quotas on the Buddhist clergy. By law, a government permit was required to be ordained as a monk or nun, and theoretically this system would serve as a means to limit the numbers of those entering the clergy. In fact, there were many monks and nuns without permits, and when the government was pressed for funds, it did not scruple to raise money by selling the 'ordination certificates' (which exempted the holder from taxes and labor services). The imperial government issued laws to restrict the flow of wealth into institutionalized Buddhism by limiting the number of temples and forbidding unauthorized private building of temples, but such laws had little practical effect because they were not enforced in any sustained, systematic way.

Not only government policy, but social attitudes among the people at large can affect the extent of religious freedom. It seems likely that the very existence of monastic institutions in Buddhism reflects the need to create a special status, recognized as set apart from the roles of worldly life, to make socially acceptable the full-time pursuit of world-transcending aims. In the minds of the laiety the existence of monks and nuns could then be justified by seeing them as specialists who embodied the religious aspiriations of the community, and who could mediate between worldly people and powers lying beyond the world, and thus benefit society as a whole.

For lay Buddhists, and even for monks and nuns, the demands of society were still a force to be reckoned with. Many Chinese monks felt obliged to make some provision for the upkeep of aged parents, and even returned home to attend to them when they fell sick. Many pious Buddhists were prevented from "leaving home" and entering the clergy by the refusal of their parents, or in the case of tenants and serfs, by the landlords to whom they were bound, to grant them permission. Buddhist laypeople had to fulfill all the customary obligations to work, pay rent and taxes, rear children, care for parents. Only the time left over from these duties was free for specifically religious endeavors. Both Zen and Pure Land teachers addressed this issue, by pointing out ways to cultivate Buddhist practices in the midst of mundane life.

The social restraints on religious freedom bore most heavily on women, as part of the general subordination of women to men in Old China. Women were not free to mingle with unrelated men, even for religious purposes. The classic complaint against the heterodox popular religions in China was that they allowed women and men to gather together without enforcing the proper distinctions. A Chinese woman who intended to follow the time-honored custom of the Zen school, travelling in search of enlightened teachers, would be met with hostility and suspicion. If a monk accepted women as disciples, slanderous gossip and accusations of immorality were inevitable. A leading Ming dynasty Zen master pointed out that it was these social restraints on women, rather than any lack of intrinsic potential for enlightenment, that made it much harder for women to advance in the Zen path.

The laws enacted at the beginning of the Ming period to restrict contacts between Buddhist clergy and laiety to ritual occasions presented a new impediment to religious freedom. The new regime desired to put a final end to the preceding period of millenarian-inspired political upheaval. The fear was that heterodox monks and nuns circulating freely among the people would spread dangerous ideas and promote political subversion. The new Ming dynasty aimed to recreating a stable social order by classifying everyone in fixed categories with obligations assigned accordingly. In this view, monks and nuns could best serve the stability of the social order in the role of ritual specialists. Those who studied Zen and the scriptures could not be trusted to say the safe thing, and the government wanted the common people insulated from unpredictable teachings.

As we have noted, the stringent early Ming regulations on Buddhist temples and clergy were probably never enforced consistently on a wide scale. The Buddhist laiety in general did not want Buddhism curbed, and there were enough influential patrons in a position to shelter Buddhist clergy and temples from the force of the law.

Even more important in keeping the Buddhist Teaching free, its adept teachers had the insight to adapt their activities to all sorts of circumstances. They were not bound by limited, limiting views: vis-a-vis secular society and culture, they were on the outside looking in. They knew how to work around as well as within social conventions. They were the consummate experts in circumventing the barriers that blocked people off from the Buddhist message. These were not only, not even mainly, the barriers of law and custom, government interference and uninformed public opinion. The greater challenge, and the more subtle achievement, was for the Buddhist teachers to pierce the barriers presented by the commonsense certainties of the unenlightened that their conditioned-in views and deluded perceptions constituted an accurate picture of reality.

8. Quality in Buddhism

In considering Buddhist history past and present, it is natural to wonder how to judge the qualitative level of Buddhism in any given time and place.

What are the hallmarks of true quality in the teaching of Buddhism? Above all, efficacy. According to all authoritative spokesmen from within the tradition, the techniques and forms through which the Dharma has been communicated were always meant as tools, as expedient means, not as dogma. Genuine Buddhist teachings were intended as provisional devices, designed to meet the specific needs. They were useful expressions of the Dharma to the extent that they were able to reach and transform the mentalities of the people of a given time and place.

The corollary is, that when particular methods and forms within Buddhism were taken as absolute standards, and venerated as sacred dogma, then genuine teaching was on the wane: the necessary adaptability had been lost, and fossilization had set in. This is why Buddhist history in all lands has been punctuated by repeated movements of renovation and reform, where new teachers emerge to tell people that the old formulations and institutions must be set aside or reworked because they are no longer serving their original purpose.

An awareness of this inner dynamic to the Buddhist teaching challenges us to look beneath the surface of the apparent ups and downs of "Buddhism" in terms of institutional wealth and wordly prestige. But this is easier said than done.

Many of the records that remain of Buddhist history invite us to focus on the superficial aspects: the numbers of monks and nuns, the splendid ornamentation of temples and monasteries, the calendar of festivals and rituals, the extent of patronage, the political and social status of Buddhist institutions, the honors and favors granted by emperors and kings.

Only in the records of the deeds and sayings of the adept teachers do we get glimpses of the person-to-person communication of the essential teaching as it was actually operating "on the ground." But by their very nature, most of the human interactions that made up the Buddhist teaching at an intimate level were not matters of record.

Here and there in the words of the enlightened teachers we also find direct comments on the qualitative state of the Buddhism of their time. When the adepts discussed the issue of quality, they identified as key factors the sincerity and dedication of the seekers, and the genuineness of the teachers. They pointed out tell-tale signs that teachers and students were not genuine: dogmatism, jealous partisanship, self-aggrandisement, mechanical adherence to certain routines.

Real teaching could not proceed when the would-be students were looking for easy gains, or seeking to have their preconceptions confirmed. Students could not make progress until they gave up their desires to experience mystical raptures, or to acquire magical powers. Students also had to abandon their previous stock of cherished opinions and incomplete interpretations of what the Dharma was.

The criteria for genuine teachers set forth by the adepts of the Zen school were very strict. To be qualified to teach Buddhism, a person had to have his or her own independent enlightenment, certified by an enlightened elder, and in addition, a thorough mastery of the theoretical and practical heritage of the Buddhist tradition. The Buddhist Teaching could not function where self-appointed "teachers" led students astray with private, fragmentary interpretations, and imposed arbitrary regimens of practice.

These time-honored Zen criteria for judging the quality of teachers and students still retain their value today.

The tell-tale signs of inauthenticity are plain to see in many manifestations of the present day imitation-Zen of the West and the fossil-Zen of the East. In plain English, putting on monastic robes, sitting cross-legged, assuming a calm manner, and memorizing a few snippets of Zen phraseology does not qualify someone to be a Zen teacher. This is as true today as it was a thousand years ago. Likewise, a sentimental longing for "spirituality" and a taste for the exotic does not automatically make someone a Zen student.

Modern people interested in Zen should be thankful that the authentic masters of the tradition were so clear in their analysis of what can go wrong with misconceived approaches to the teaching. We should heed their warnings. Sectarian biases, blind adherence to inherited routines, dogmatism, putting on airs of wisdom and mystery, power trips and mind games: these are clear signals that the "Zen followers" in question are rank pretenders.

III. A Map of Zen Mind

According to the traditional formula, Zen points directly to the human mind, without establishing any verbal formulations as sacred, in order to enable people to see their real identity and become enlightened.

One way to acquaint modern readers with the basic outlook of the Zen school is to describe what the term 'mind' meant to Zen Buddhists. The word 'mind' occurs constantly in Zen writings, and by exploring its meanings we can see how the Zen school saw enlightenment and how they proposed for us to reach it.

1. Buddha Mind and the Human Mind

In Zen discourse, the word 'mind' is used in two basic senses.

On the one hand, 'mind' means the mentality of ordinary unenlightened human beings, the so-called 'mind of delusion'. This is the mind that is shaped by one's upbringing and culture, the mind that has been conditioned by the circumstances and formative influences to which people are exposed throughout their lives. This mind is governed by patterns of aversion and attraction that dictate one's values and preferences and choices. It is both limited and limiting. 'Mind' in this sense is both the product of karma, of the actions of oneself and others, and the source of further actions, more karma, so it is also known as 'karmic consciousness'.

On the other hand, in Zen discourse the word 'mind' also refers to the enlightened mind, the Buddha-mind, the one absolute reality underlying all particular contingent phenomena. This mind is omnipresent, everywhere-equal, omniscient, changeless, eternal, infinite. All the buddhas, all the enlightened ones, share in the experience of it. Even the unenlightened, though they are unaware of it, are not outside it. This is 'Mind' with a capital M.

To us, the unenlightened, these two meanings for the word 'mind' seem to be poles apart: the human mind vs. the mind of the Tao, finite mind vs. infinite mind, false mind vs. true mind, particular mind vs. universal mind, the conditioned mind of delusion vs. the absolute mind of God, the Buddha-mind.

But according to the Buddhist teaching, this dualism is only apparent, a figment of false consciousness. There is no ontological separation between the human mind and the Buddha-mind, because the Buddha-mind is the ground of being for all phenomena, including the perceptual worlds of unenlightened human beings. This is what gives us the possibility of enlightenment. In practice, the aim of all Buddhist techniques is to reawaken humans to their real identity as buddhas, to restore their awareness of their intrinsic link to the Buddha-mind, to bridge the gulf that unenlightened people ordinarily experience between the two levels of mind. Therefore, the double sense of the term 'mind' in Zen served as a convenient means for indicating the fundamental continuity between the human mind and the Buddha-mind.

2. Analyzing the Human Mind

Through the ages Buddhist theorists gave close attention to the make-up and functioning of the ordinary human mind. They examined in detail the processes by which the human mind is conditioned and shaped into the self-centered configuration characteristic of ordinary worldly people, for whom all awareness of their original link to the Buddha-mind is blocked off. From personal experience, they knew that human beings are capable of far more than the temporary satisfactions and precarious complacency of a life driven by pain and pleasure and arbitrary meanings and artificial self-definitions.

The Zen school took over the analysis of human consciousness advanced by the Yogacara tradition of Indian Buddhist philosophy. The Yogacara adepts made the observation that ordinarily, people do not directly perceive the world-as-it-is, but rather project upon the world of form and consciousness a system of mental representations (in Sanskrit: vijnapti) constructed according to the conditioning with which their minds have been imprinted. Instead of perceiving the phenomenal world as it is, a ceaseless flux of cause-and-effect, people reify the categories they project upon it, and insist upon the reality of the imagined entities their own definitions create.

This fundamental axiom of the Yogacara analysis is not unlike the observations of twentieth century anthropology and linguistics on the decisive role of language and culture in shaping perception. Every person with cosmopolitan experience is aware of cross-cultural differences that confirm this basic point. Everyone who has travelled in various countries knows that the spices which people in one culture find delicious, average people from another culture might find painfully pungent or even totally disgusting. Everyone knows that the same sounds which speakers of one language hear as perfectly distinct, speakers of another language might find impossible to tell apart.

Though such observations are common knowledge in our cosmopolitan modern world, people commonly resist the implications of these incontrovertible facts. Armed with his dogmatic commonsense, the ordinary man in the street in all cultures, whether educated or not, is fully convinced that his own perceptions accurately reflect objective outer realities. When pressed on this point, he can quickly appeal to the consensus of his fellows, who all of course share the conventions of his own culture: case closed.

So even for most "modern" people, including the intelligentsia who theoretically should know better, any sustained focus on the conditioned, conventional nature of their own perceptions remains taboo. They proceed through life guiding their actions by whatever standards their community has taught them to accept as their own. In a pluralistic society, without a single, unanimously accepted set of values, they can flatter themselves all the more that they have freely chosen what they believe on the basis of their experience of reality. No one cares to notice how circumscribed is the range of options upon which this "free choice" operates. People are sure they have "made up their own minds" (about what to believe and how to act) on the basis of the facts.

But from the Buddhist point of view, it is precisely this sense of certainty, this insistence that one's own conventional notions of reality *are* reality (and the parallel fiction that they are one's own), is the linchpin of delusion. This may be why, when they are exposed to Buddhist ideas on this subject, the defenders of conventional thinking in all cultures, from classical India to medieval China to the modern West, have found Buddhism so irritating, and so threatening.

The Yogacara analysis distinguishes eight kinds of consciousness. They are separated out for purposes of analysis, but in life they function together simultaneously to produce a person's experience.

The first five consciousnesses are associated with what we call the five senses: sight, hearing, taste, touch, and smell. Sensory experience is comprised of the sense organ, the corresponding sense object, and the associated consciousness: for example, sight = eye + form + visual consciousness; hearing = ear + sound + auditory consciousness.

The sixth consciousness is the conceptual faculty, which classifies and categorizes sense-data into recognized entities, in ways influenced by the training a person receives growing up in and acting as a member of a particular community and culture.

The seventh consciousness functions to evaluate what is experienced by the first six consciousnesses. It imposes judgments in terms of good and bad, right and wrong, desirable and undesirable, and thus creates motivations to action. It too is shaped in each person by the conditioning patterns of upbringing and culture.

The eighth consciousness is known as the storehouse consciousness. It is the repository of all the impressions that accumulate over the course of a person's life. This furnishes the stock of images and concepts and mental habits through which the person orders experience.

It is easy to cite examples of the way the same phenomenon is perceived differently by different people, depending on the different categories employed by the sixth consciousness, the divergent evaluations made by the seventh consciousness, and the different stock of impressions available from each person's storehouse consciousness. It becomes obvious that these factors are decisive determinants of perception.

Consider a work of modern art, a nonfigurative painting. First take the level of the sixth consciousness. To a peasant in the hinterland of China it appears as a strange and meaningless jumble of color. The average unsophisticated Westerner only knows it is some sort of modern art. The art connoisseur immediately recognizes it as the well-known work X by artist Y bearing the familiar traits of the Z movement.

At the level of the seventh consciousness, each perceiver judges the painting differently. To the peasant, the nonfigurative painting is simply incoherent; if he is told that it is art, he may scoff or doubt the sanity of the artist. The average Westerner, though he knows the work is intended as art, may evaluate it in a similar way, as nonsense or madness. If he has had enough schooling, and is away from the comfortable company of his peers, he might very well keep his opinions to himself, knowing that they will be taken as a mark of his own lack of sophistication. The art connoisseur will have the most complex evaluation of the work: he may think X is not as good as other works by the artist Y, or prefer Y's contemporary artist Q, or place X in context of the whole movement Z.

Considering the level of the eighth consciousness, we can see the basis for each person's varying experience of the painting. The peasant is stumped by the abstract painting, because there is no analogy to it in his experience. The average Westerner can only fit it into a vague general concept of 'modern art' which to him all looks more or less alike. The connoisseur, who has accumulated many detailed impressions of modern painting in his storehouse consciousness, can match it against a more systematically ordered range of images.

It is easy to imagine other examples where the perception of the modern sophisticate cannot compare in depth and nuance to the perception of the peasant. Let them take a walk in the fields. The city-dweller, for all his schooling, cannot tell millet from wheat: all he knows is that he is looking at some kind of plant. The peasant's perception is much more detailed: he knows what grain it is, and what variety, and how far along it is, and can judge the quality of the soil and the season's weather from looking at the condition of the plants.

Again, it is obvious that the peasant's and the city-dweller's perceptions of "the same" plants differ completely, depending on the different contents of their sixth, seventh, and eighth consciousnesses.

The distinction among the eight modes of consciousness is an analytical device. In moment-to-moment experience all eight levels of consciousness operate at once intertwined with each other. A person's experience of sights, sounds, odors, tastes, and physical contacts is shaped by the categorizations and judgments given by the sixth and seventh consciousness, and modeled by the stored impressions contained in the eighth consciousness. The sixth, seventh, and eighth consciousnesses take on particular configurations in each person, molded by the cultural and social circumstances that surround them, and determined by their own life-histories.

3. From Theory to Practice

The aim of the adepts of the Zen school was to put the Yogacara analysis of consciousness to the practical use for which it was intended by its originators.

The techniques taught by the Zen masters were designed to liberate the human mind from the limitations imposed on perception by the sixth and seventh consciousnesses, and gradually to purify the eighth consciousness of its accumulated stereotypes.

In Zen teaching, the sixth and seventh consciousnesses are seen as the keys to the process of delusion, by which the mentality of ordinary human beings is narrowed down to it exclusive focus on conventional reality, and screened from an awareness of the Buddha-mind. It is through them that the false consciousness of a self separated from others is created, and the self-centered view of the world is maintained. Through them, people are deprived of their birthright of enlightenment, and enclosed within a world of arbitrary discriminations, to revolve in routines of seeking what they have been programmed to desire and avoiding what they have been trained to dislike.

Some Zen techniques worked over the long run, to reorder and refine the sixth and seventh consciousnesses, to rearrange conceptual categories and shift patterns of judgment and motivation. The cumulative effect would be to empty the storehouse consciousness of the seeds of ignorant action. Other Zen methods worked in the moment, to temporarily suspend the activities of the sixth and seventh consciousnesses, to break the spell of their obsessive categorizing and evaluating, in order to let a wider reality emerge into the awareness of the practitioner.

Both kinds of techniques were commonly used in the Zen school, in many forms. They were employed as expedient means, as tools to refine the human mind and allow it to rediscover its intrinsic link to the Buddha-mind. Zen teachers were likened to skilled physicians, because their task was to diagnose the particular configuration of deluded perception and conduct afflicting the learner, and to prescribe the appropriate methods in a timely fashion so that they could work effectively.

Many Zen people had "left home" and become monks and nuns. They were renunciants, who did not participate in the ordinary social roles, or seek the ordinary worldly satisfactions. Instead, they were supposed to follow a rigorous course of discipline, curbing their desires, dressing and eating simply, refraining from sexual relations, and working hard at meditation and their other tasks. They abandoned the competition for wealth, honor, and position, to live as part of a community of religious seekers and faithfully serve and follow the instructions of qualified teachers.

The austere style of life of Zen monks and nuns was not meant as an end in itself, but as a means to gradually reorient values and motivations. In other words, it was a method of purifying the seventh consciousness. For those who ultimately succeeded in becoming detached from worldly desires, the strict discipline and asceticism had served the purpose and might be put aside.

Some Zen people remained in lay life, but this was considered a much more difficult path. Here people would be exposed to all the entanglements of the ordinary world, and old habits of mind would be harder to break. To achieve detachment and clear wisdom and unsentimental compassion while surrounded by people freely indulging in worldly motivations was considered a magnificent achievement, and the enlightened laypeople recorded in the annals of the Zen school were particularly venerated.

Whether as home-leavers or householders, by renouncing the pursuit of worldly pleasures and abandoning ordinary expectations and ambitions, Zen people aimed to break the hold of selfish desires over their perceptions and actions. Reorienting the seventh consciousness in this way was meant to open the way for the development of more enlightened views in which all phenomena are seen as equal and nothing is sought or shunned.

The taking of vows played a major role in Zen as well as in other forms of Buddhism. By taking vows, Buddhists marked their dedication to a fundamental restructuring of their whole pattern of motivations and judgments, that is, of their seventh consciousness. Mahayana Buddhists would vow to follow the bodhisattva path. To be a bodhisattva, or 'enlightening being', is the ideal of Mahayana Buddhism as a whole, and naturally of Zen as well. The bodhisattva vows to achieve enlightenment not only for herself or himself, but for all living beings, and undertakes to remain in the world after enlightenment working tirelessly for the liberation of all beings. The aim of Zen people was not to escape from the world, but to achieve the kind of detachment and insight that would enable them to become immune to worldly entanglements, so they could function in the world with disinterested compassion.

The study of the Buddhist literature was another method commonly used in the Zen school to rearrange the seventh consciousness and to add new impressions to the storehouse consciousness.

The Buddhist sutras present vivid pictures of the unimaginably vast, multilevel, intercommunicating reality experienced by the enlightened. The whole enterprise of the teaching and attainment of enlightenment is shown taking place in countless worlds among all manner of beings. Ordinary barriers of time and space and self and other are transcended in the accounts of the visionary manifestations of the buddhas.

The Buddhist philosophical treatises, called shastras, use logical argument and analytic categories to establish alternative interpretations of cognition and reality that decisively refute the conventional common-sense viewpoint. They show the contradictions and conundrums to which a naive reliance on language as the supposed reflection of reality leads. They analyse human perception to show the unreal, constructed nature of basic categories like subject and object. They provide conceptual maps for the transformation of ordinary human consciousness into the wisdom of the buddhas.

The Zen school produced its own extensive literature, distilling the wisdom of the sutras and shastras, and restating the teaching of Buddhism in a new key. There were extensive biographical collections that provided role models for a way of life beyond worldly convention. Zen poetry showed reality in a new light with a special blend of haunting metaphors and unexpected turns of thought. There were also the recorded talks and letters of Zen teachers giving Buddhist lessons in blunt, pungent, down-to-earth language, directly challenging readers to make the great work of Buddhism their own personal task, and providing pointers to the Path.

Practitioners in the Zen school also employed many techniques specifically designed to work on the sixth consciousness, to interrupt its obsessive categorizing activity, and to loosen its stranglehold on perception. Ordinarily the sixth consciousness maintains an internal dialogue that in effect censors experience and forces everything into preconceived, familiar categories. By suspending the operation of the sixth consciousness, and moving outside the confines of its routine judgments, the person's mind is opened up to te possibility of other forms of more direct, more comprehensive awareness.

Many forms of meditation were used in the Zen school. After all, the word "Zen" (in Chinese, *chan*; in Vietnamese, *thien*; in Korean *son*) is based on the Sanskrit word *dhyana*, which means "meditation".

One method was to allow the internal dialogue of the sixth consciousness to die down by simply dropping thoughts as soon as they arose, not trying to stop them, but not following along with them either. This is simple to describe, but hard at first to do, since it involves breaking with a familiar habit of stringing together an interior life of loosely connected wandering thoughts. Like other forms of meditation, proficiency comes with sustained effort.

In other forms of meditation, the practitioner would concentrate on various aspects of reality emphasized in the Buddhist teachings. Particular meditation perspectives in this vein were found to be useful were: the interdependence of subject and object; the interconnected nature of all things, and the process of interdependent causation that takes phenomena into and out of existence; the way all phenomena lack independent, permanent, fixed identities; the mean between the identity-lessness of all phenomena and their relative existence.

People meditating might also put their attention on particular focal points, in lieu of the habitual internal dialogue of the sixth consciousness. The focal points used included: the movement of the breath, particular colors and sounds, images of buddhas and bodhi-sattvas, mandalas and mantras.

Chanting mantras and reciting sutras were techniques for loosening the grip of the sixth consciousness. By repeating the set of syllables of the mantra again and again with the attention focused on them, or by intently reciting the words of a sutra, the sixth consciousness was brought to a halt. With the usual internal dialogue interrupted, the limiting description of the world it maintains also ceases, and the wider reality can come into view.

Many people incorporated the buddha-name recitation of Pure Land Buddhism into their Zen practice. In Zen usage, chanting the buddha-name was a way to focus the mind on Buddha: a moment of pure mindfulness of Buddha *is* the Pure Land. Another prevalent method that combined Zen and Pure Land practices was this: when recitation of Amitabha's name was strongly established, the focus was shifted to the question, "Who is the one reciting the buddha-name?"

The Zen school had a special stock of sayings and stories which were used as focal points in meditation. These were known as *hua-tou* '[meditation] sayings' or *gong-an* 'public cases' (perhaps more familiar in English in the Japanese reading *koan*) or *yin-yuan* '[stories of] the causes and conditions [of enlightenment]'. The public cases contained multilevel semantics, designed first to intrigue the sixth consciousness and engage it in figuring out 'the meaning', then tease and frustrate it, then derailing the sixth consciousness altogether in order to create an impact on the mind beyond the level of intellectual comprehension.

With intense effort by the practitioner in keeping attention focused on the meditation case, its many levels of meaning would gradually open up. Over time, contact with the public cases eventually shifts the sixth consciousness out of its routinized habits and proclivity for facile judgments.

Using unsettling metaphors and apparent paradoxes, the public cases cryptically encode various aspects of the message of the Buddha Dharma. They are abstract structures containing basic lessons, and serve as signposts pointing to the truth from all directions.

By the time of Shiqi, there were several famous collections of meditation cases in circulation in the Zen communities. The famous *gong-an* were indeed 'public cases', well known in Zen circles, with accumulating layers of prose and verse commentaries and added remarks. Western readers can consult our translation of the most famous of the *gong-an* collections, the *Blue Cliff Record*, to discover for themselves the intricacy, beauty, and depth of this classic Zen form.

All these methods, and many more, were the practical tools of the Zen school, the medicines Zen teachers prescribed as needed to cure their students of the habitual attitudes and preconceptions of the worldly mentality. They were intended to "untie the bonds and dissolve the sticking points" of ordinary consciousness, and open the way for people to recover their real identities, their inherent enlightened nature.

4. Transforming Consciousness into Wisdom

The Yogacara theory of consciousness had a practical intent, which is why it proved so useful to the Zen school. The Yogacara analysis of ordinary conditioned consciousness leads directly into a description of enlightenment and an account of the attributes of buddhahood.

In Yogacara terminology, the ultimate goal of Buddhist practices is the transformation of consciousness into wisdom: the transformation of the eight consciousnesses through which the unenlightened perceive the world into the four liberative wisdoms of the buddhas. It is these four wisdoms which give the buddhas their ability to perceive reality as it is, and to act for the enlightenment of all beings.

"Reality as it is" encompasses a complex totality, according to the Buddhist teaching. It includes all manifestations of phenomenal reality and the laws of cause and effect governing them, as well as the one, everywhere-equal absolute reality which is the true nature of phenomenal reality and its ground of being. Phenomenal reality spans not only the patterns of matter and energy we customarily think of as inanimate physical objects and processes, but also the sensory faculties and factors of consciousness that occur in sentient beings. Thus the totality of reality also includes all the systems of mental representations sentient beings of all kinds project upon the phenomenal world, all their private worlds of subjective experience.

In the enlightened ones, the buddhas, a "transformation of the basis" of experience takes place. A buddha no longer assembles his or her personal experience on the basis of the limited stock of images contained in his or her individual storehouse consciousness. Instead, in a buddha, the eighth consciousness is transformed into the "Mirror-like Wisdom", which contains all possible manifestations of form and consciousness like images reflected in a mirror. Whatever phenomenal manifestations appear in it, the Mirror Wisdom remains pure and clear and unchanging and untouched.

In a buddha, the seventh consciousness is transformed into what is known as the "Equality Wisdom". In place of the arbitrary, parochial judgments and evaluations of the seventh consciousness, based on the conditioning the person has received, the Equality Wisdom directly perceives the true reality of all phenomena, their absolute essence, which is universal and everywhere equal. Equipped with the Equality Wisdom, the enlightened being is capable of the equanimity needed to cope with deluded beings without being drawn into or repelled by their delusion. The Equality Wisdom is the key to the tireless, detached compassion of the bodhisattvas, who view self and others as one, and who experience nirvana right in the midst of the afflictions and passions of cyclical existence. The bodhisattva can take on the endless task of leading all sentient beings to ultimate enlightenment, fortified with direct knowledge via the Equality Wisdom that in essence all beings are already one with absolute reality.

In ordinary people, the sixth consciousness classifies all experience according to the familiar categories they have been trained to accept as real. Each system of conditioning the sixth consciousness, each language and cultural tradition, emphasizes certain features and defines other parts of reality out of existence, and thereby produces biases and blind-spots that limit freedom of action and inhibit adaptability. In buddhas, the sixth consciousness is transformed into the "Analytical Wisdom." Through the Analytical Wisdom, the buddhas accurately perceive the true pattern of cause and effect operating in the phenomenal world. This enables them to see into the process of delusion and analyse the formation of the false consciousness that traps sentient beings. With this insight, the buddhas are able to devise teachings and practical techniques that are appropriate to the needs of particular sentient beings, in order to liberate them from their bonds of ignorance.

The first five consciousnesses in ordinary people are associated with the life of the senses. In buddhas, these consciousnesses are trans-formed into the "Accomplishment of Works Wisdom". This is the medium for the physical participation of the buddhas in the worlds of sentient beings. It is the wisdom through which the salvific works of the buddhas are enacted, through which the skillful means of teaching devised by the Analytical Wisdom are given concrete form and carried out.

The four wisdoms illustrate the unity of absolute and relative in the experiential realm of the enlightened. This is the underlying principle of the Buddhist philosophy of being and the basic condition which makes enlightenment possible for all sentient beings. The Mirror Wisdom represents the omnipresent, absolute Buddha-Mind containing all relative, localized, particular phenomena, including the mentalities and subjective experiences of sentient beings. The Equality Wisdom reveals that all these relative phenomena in turn contain the one absolute reality as their essence. The Analytical Wisdom and the Accomplishment of Works Wisdom represent the liberating work through which the Buddha-Mind reveals itself to human minds, or in other words, through which the absolute takes particular form and communicates itself to the relative.

5. Yogacara Theory and Zen

This Yogacara analysis of consciousness, and of the transformation of consciousness into wisdom, may appear to be an exercise in abstract philosophy, but it is far more than that. In fact, it is a map, drawn by those who have been there, charting the inconceivable. Buddhist philosophy is not an attempt to arrive at truth by a process of analytical categories and reasoning. Rather, it is a means for those with direct experience of truth to communicate truth to those who have not yet known it in its totality. It is meant to provide a conceptual map for those still in the meshes of conditioned consciousness to enable them to see the way out of their dilemma.

Those who study Zen will be able to interpret Zen metaphors and comprehend Zen practices more accurately by locating them within the Yogacara analysis of consciousness and its transformation into wisdom. The Yogacara teachers and the Zen adepts have left us with a detailed map of the journey from the human mind to the Buddha-Mind: it is still up to us to make the trip.

Teachings of Zen Master Shiqi Xinyue "Stone River"

1. The Ready-Made Case (To Mr. Yuan)

The ready-made public case—how could it depend on verbal explanations? If you hesitate and entrust yourself to your private biases, when a target is born, it attracts arrows. If you travel in a dream through bounded realms, you will not avoid obliviously wasting your time and wandering around aimlessly. You will abandon your family and lose your livelihood.

Suddenly you feel sorry and have a moment of insight. But succeeding in turning yourself around is not a sudden accomplishment. The knife pares away, the water washes clean. [Despite your gradual practice, to you] mind seems hidden, vague: you seem to remember, you seem to forget. This defeat is even more serious.

Mr. Yuan, you have dragged your dream south with you. You want to find a phrase that will assist you in developing insight. So I take the hammer of the polar mountain to beat on the drum of empty space. But I'm afraid I am still unable to call you [from your dream].

Because you are asleep, without being fully aware of [what's going on], you cannot get yourself going. One day when you are going through the clouds crossing a stream, as you lose your footing on level ground, the eye will open by itself. Only then can you probe the tiger's lair on South Mountain, and pass through the dragon gate.

First get a firm hold on [the dragon's] throat, and do not let it turn to the side: only then can you pluck out the claws and teeth and play with the horns. Otherwise, as soon as you meet the [dragon's] mouth, you'll lose your life totally. In that case, though [grappling with the dragon of reality] is called a good cause, it brings about a bad result.

NOTES

"Public case" The Zen *koan*: stories and scenes and sayings epitomizing the message of Zen, used as meditation topics. Reality itself at all levels provides a "ready-made case."

"The tiger's lair" where enlightened teachers dwell.

"The dragon gate" where "fish" (ordinary people) are transformed into "dragons" (enlightened people).

2. Zen Lore   (Excerpts from a letter to Attendant Yuan)

In the old days when Yaoshan inquired about the Path from Nanyue, and he first heard the saying "Thus or otherwise: neither will do", he was like a mosquito on an iron ox [unable to bite into it]. [Later] when it came to [Yaoshan saying] "I do not do a single thing—quiet sitting is doing something", he was like a gourd floating on the water: he could not be held down. He just had his skin totally stripped off, but he did not know that his true reality was still there. [Later on Yaoshan's disciple] drew in those who follow the waves by saying "I was at Yaoshan's for thirty years and he just illuminated this matter [of enlightenment]." [With this disciple, Yaoshan] planted wheat but produced beans. Check it out: where was his defeat?

The first patriarch in India called to the second patriarch and said, "Take down the flag in front of the temple gate [and put up your own: you are ready to succeed me]." Yongquan said, "At forty, I still got bent out of shape." Xianglin said, "Only at forty did I achieve oneness."
"Without leaving Flying Monkey Range, this eye penetrates the nine heavens." "Without coming down from Fisher Mountain, this energy engulfs the four oceans." Mr. Bei and Mr. Hui [who uttered these sayings] were from different times and different regions, but one indictment covers their crime [of clinging to oneness]. Why didn't [Mr. Bei] who "broke up his family and scattered his household at eighteen" get old without stopping and resting? Did he not spend his money for straw sandals [for his travels in quest of enlightenment] in vain? If you say, "Through the misty waters of a hundred towns, what going, what coming? Over ten thousand miles of mountains and rivers, it's above and below my feet," I'm afraid this itself is the fork in the road.

Some talk Zen to great lengths, but do they know the scene of planting the fields to provide a lot to eat? Do those who plant the fields to provide a lot to eat know the principles involved in talking Zen to great lengths? If we do not casually let them go, [we must communicate the whole message], not only one or two principles and ideas.
Attendant Yuan of Pujiang, you seek some words to return to your home village with, so you present me with five sheets of Chen-qiao parchment [to write on]. When you return to your home temple, do not chew them up. Not only are they without flavor, but they'll flay your insides.

NOTES

"A mosquito on an iron ox" The ordinary mind of people, bound by environmental influences and conditioning, cannot penetrate true reality, which is infinite and inconceivable.

"The fork in the road" The aim of Zen, having realized the oneness of all phenomena, is to be able to function in the world of differentiation as an enlightening being.

3. How to Serve Buddha   (To Reverend Yuan)

A verse says:

> The top of a hundred foot pole
> That side of the bridge across the mountain torrent
> The lame donkey loses its footing
> The eye of your true self suddenly opens

Another verse:

> I have a bright pearl
> Long locked up amidst sensory afflictions
> Today the sensory dusts are gone and the light is born
> Shining through the myriad crags of the green mountains

I sigh for the Master of Mt. Yu in Chaling: wherever he went he always shook his bells. When he strummed his tongue to utter mantras, was he not a bright pearl emitting light?

When the hand slips and the foot falters, as you grunt [in surprise], it appears whole before your eyes in every particular.

What about later? Reverend Yuan, you are well able to study it in detail. Between ancient and modern there's not a hairsbreadth [of difference]. So wherever you are, take the straightforward mind as your site of enlightenment, take straightforward conduct as your work to serve Buddha, take straightforward speech as your true repentance, and use straightforward action to add power and maintain it.

If you act otherwise, you are falsely cheating yourself, and you are someone with whom the buddhas and Zen masters do not associate. If you say there is some other advantage to this, I am not aware of it.

I know this longwinded talk of mine will not avoid a laugh from Chaling.

NOTES

"The top of a hundred foot pole" At the peak of meditative concentration, with the mind focussed on oneness.

"That side of the rushing torrent" Absolute reality, which subsumes all differences and distinctions.

"The lame donkey" The discriminating intellect and the motivations arising from it; the questing mentality of the seeker.

"A bright pearl" Buddha-nature, our real identity, endowed with inherent wisdom and compassion.

"Mantras" Sounds recited to focus the mind and align it with reality.

4: Impact   (To Attendant Liaozhe)

The intent of our teaching is like a poison-smeared drum. Once it is beaten, those who hear it, near and far, all perish. That those who hear it perish is surely true. But what about the deaf people?

Xuefeng asked Deshan, "How has the work of the school been passed on since antiquity?" Deshan hit him a blow with the staff and said, "What are you saying?" The next day, Xuefeng asked for instruction, and Deshan said, "Our school has no words and phrases, and there is not a single dharma to give to people." When Xuefeng heard this, [the feelings he held within] his breast emptied out: it was like the bottom falling out of a bucket.

When the other experts of the Zen school who had the great eye [of enlightenment] showed a device or imparted a saying, those who heard went deaf, and those who saw were awestruck. Some rubbed their palms and laughed. Some held up their hands and waved them around. Some stretched out and ran toward it. With some, both knees spontaneously buckled. These are all cases of perishing at the sound of the [poison-smeared Dharma] drum.

There is only one reason for this: will and energy align, mind and attention are concentrated. In everything everywhere you can wholly let go, wholly take charge, wholly roll up or roll out, wholly receive the use of it. It is like standing on the summit of the polar mountain.

Unless you are like this, the eye [of enlightenment] has not opened. Once the eye opens, then what is all around you—the four continents, the sun, moon, and stars, the mountains, rivers, and the whole earth— this is all one reality that lies at your feet. If your vantage point is not loftly, then you will not avoid going back and forth in a petty way between far and near and high and low. The fork in the road will go along with you, and you will never get done.

Excellent people have a correct causal basis and true faith. They achieve special excellence of body and mind, and approach teachers and spiritual friends of excellence. They keep at it for months and years, not worrying that anything will be left unachieved, not worrying that they will not share in this affair [of enlightenment] with all the former generations of elders.

If you are sometimes illuminated and sometimes in the dark, if you take a half step forward and two steps back, if you babble on and fly around in confusion, if you emerge and then sink back into the stinking bag [of illusion]—if [in this condition] you hope for a moment of Accord [with reality], even a hundred beats of the poison-smeared drum will be to no avail.

Talking like this is the secondary level. Believing this talk is the tertiary level. If you hear it like wind passing through the treetops, like water wearing away the rock of ages, I am sure you have already witnessed this samadhi with the Buddha King of Emptiness. Could this be easily attained?

Attendant Liaozhe has been in the assembly at North Mountain for a long time working on this Path. For his visit to Xicheng, he seeks some words, so I have written this as an admonitory aid.

NOTES

"The polar mountain" Mount Sumeru, the great mountain at the center of the world in the classical Indian cosmology adopted by Buddhism, surrounded by the four continents.

"Samadhi" Stable meditative concentration.

5: It's All Here Now   (To Zen man Nian)

"It is not the wind-bell ringing: it is our minds ringing." "It is not the wind or the flag moving: it is your minds moving." How special! This is the stick that the ancestral teachers in China and India used to beat the grass to frighten snakes. Have you washed out your ears and eyes in these sayings?

Two thousand years ago, ten thousand miles away—it's all here now. Wherever we step is our home mountain. Whatever strikes our ears and eyes is our one true self. The hundreds and thousands and tens of thousands and hundreds of millions [of different things] are all our one intimate retinue. The many and varied teachers we have learned from are all our one enlightened teacher. From the first, there has never been any difference between China and India, between this and that. How could there be any difference between Wu and Shu [opposite ends of China], between going or coming?

The moment you stop and observe, China is China and India is India. Rivers and mountains stretch in all directions and cities and towers rise up everywhere. When a slight breeze blows through, the banner moves and the bells tinkle. The eyes see and the ears hear— a thousand hands cannot cover them. But at this moment, all of this cannot fool [the awake person] one bit. Didn't the early sages say it? "Today I entrust this affar to you: never let it be in vain."

Zen man Nian is returning home to attend on his aged tutor. Thinking there wouldn't be the trouble of saying a fond farewell, I gladly wrote this to give him.

6: Thought & No-Thought
(To Zen man Si, *si* as in *siliang* 'thought')

This Dharma is not something that can be understood by discriminating thought. [I ask you] high-class guests who study the mystery, what do you call 'This Dharma'? Here you should utter a turning word that cuts off ancient and modern and makes everyone not fall into discriminating thought, so that they can all understand totally. If there is the least bit of lag, then you are within [the ambit of] discriminating thought, dreaming.

Haven't you seen Guishan's saying? "By thinking about the wonder of no-thought, we turn thought back to the inexhaustibility of the flames of spiritual awareness. With thought ended, we return to the source, where real nature and surface forms are equal, where true pattern and apparent phenomena are not two, where the real buddha is thusness as it is."

Though not without profound talk that enters into inner truth, what is Guishan so casually calling 'the real buddha'? Are there false buddhas? What turning word can you utter here, to avoid lumping together real nature & surface form, true pattern & apparent phenomena, and thought & no-thought, and leaving yourself no place to stick your head out?

If you do not agree, look again at Yangshan's trailing vines. "To know by thinking falls into the secondary. To know without thinking falls into the tertiary."

Yangshan is not lacking in a unique eye that transcends the Zen school. But when Yangshan knows by thinking, what does he know? What turning word can you put here to avoid falling into the secondary or tertiary?

Officially, not even a needle is allowed through, but to repay the benevolence we go to the spreading tendrils of the trailing vines. To know by thinking puts a film over the eyes. To know without thinking blinds the eyes. If you put a film over the eyes, blue sky on flat ground. If you blind the eyes, oxen run and tigers glower.

Although here we have conversation that falls into the weeds, in essence, "It is easy to be filled up on coarse food, and if you chew it up fine it's hard to go hungry." You should work on this, Mr. Si.

NOTES

"Trailing vines" Verbal explanations of the inconceivable Buddha Dharma; attempted rationalizations, which, like trailing vines, tend to spread out endlessly, reaching no real conclusion.

7: There is no other road   (To Zhao Jiyan)

Zhao Jiyan of Guanghan has brought rigor to the declining discipline in the garden of the Zen ancestors. Now he suddenly talks of returning home, and I forcefully try to keep him from leaving. So I quote for him what Prajnatara, the Twenty-Seventh Patriarch of Zen in India, said [to his successor, Bodhidharma]: "Though China is broad, there is no other road. You must make provisional use of it for your descendents to walk upon."

This verse is a net that spreads over the sky. Before the sun has washed, it takes the world of true elixir and captures its totality with one cast of the net. All the people ancient and modern who have awakened to the source are unable to pass through this net—it's not just the greatest adepts like Deshan and Baizhang.

People in these later days who put their bodies in the Zen community are the stupidest in the whole world. They may not know [the Buddha Dharma] exists. If they do know, they do not practice it. If they do practice, eight or nine out of ten do not get anywhere. The garden of the Zen ancestors is collapsing: the altar of the Zen school is overgrown and wild. The sandalwood forest of former times, the garden of sweet dew, today is a thicket of thorns stretching to the horizon, where foxes and rabbits cross paths.

Can this not be the fault of those who have occupied the teachers' seats and taken charge of the Great Dharma? Is it not the fault of those who go restlessly from one Zen community to the next?

NOTES

"Provisional use" The teachings of the Buddhist tradition were considered not as final truths or dogmas (because the Dharma transcends all formulations), but rather as expedient methods suited to the capacities of those to whom they were addressed, to lead them to the whole truth. Because the Dharma is inconceivable, its teachers have no choice but to use temporary expedients to communicate it.

"True elixir" A Taoist term used in the Zen school as a metaphor for the techniques used to enable people to open up their enlightened perception.

8: How to Learn Zen   (To Zen man Hui of Da-zhou)

With [genuine] patchrobed monks, the eye on the end of the staff is correct, and from under their straw sandals, a wind is born. They leave one Zen community, enter another, one where one [enlightened] person is, one where a half [enlightened] person is. They square their shoulders in the direction they are going, and observe the wind to set their sails. What's right they extend, and what's wrong they cut away. The reed cushion and meditation brace are their good friends wherever they are. For them the forest of thorns and the unbreakable trap have a fine flavor. With enlightened teachers checking them and reproving them, they go for months and years being polished and honed.

When they lose their footing and topple over, the whole face is revealed. Some throw away their staves. Some pick up a winnowing basket. Over a myriad ages of rivers and mountains, in one morning of windy moonlight, with each and every step they take they meet *Him* everywhere. They sit inert and oblivious, apparently lifeless but satisfied.

With sparks struck from stone or a flash of lightning, a blink of the eye is still slow. When the blue heavens thunder, there's no time to cover your ears. The old adepts of the various regions are all masters of the family style: they stand independently and walk alone, transmitting the Dharma of their family.

When the great adepts-to-be met their teachers, the mind-tracks were obvious, like parallel lines that could be picked out. If lofty gentlemen go travelling [to 'study Zen'] without taking the ancient sages as their model and without undertaking real in-person study, then they are said to be "blind men without the eye of wisdom" who "follow the waves and abandon the source". Think about it!

NOTES

"The eye on the end of the staff" Symbolizing the sincere student's power to discern which influences are really conducive to enlightenment, and to guide his search accordingly.

"A wind is born" Here wind symbolizes the transformative power of genuine intent.

"Patched robe" Symbol of the Zen people, as of the Sufis.

"Forest of thorns, unbreakable trap" The teaching devices of the Zen school, which at once intrigue and confound the intellect, and foster the development of nonconceptual wisdom.

"The whole face" of reality, of Dharmakaya Buddha.

Him Dharmakaya Buddha, absolute reality.

"Family style" The teaching style and conduct of the Zen masters. Various lineages of closely related Zen adepts had their own characteristic styles.

9: Worker-Monks   (To estate supervisor Quan)

[Among the eminent enlightened teachers,] Huangmei carried the weight of a mortar [hulling rice] for eight months. Niutou hauled rice day after day. Some worked burning over the fields. Some guided the plows. Some carried hoes. Some worked with spades. Some split firewood for the stove, some fetched water to irrigate the vegetables. In recent times, [monks] have acted as millers and harvest supervisors. All [these endeavors] exemplify the luminous, earth-shaking model of the ancient buddhas: "A day without work, a day without food."

Although I am not talented, I have tried [to act like this]. Now I live at a small temple, where my elder brother Quan takes care of affairs. He is consistent and straightforward, and does not scheme to impress people.

But to become a truly great man, things which ought to be done should be done thoroughly and painstakingly from beginning to end, so there is no shame before the ancients.

I send my prayers and salutations.

Also, to give him a friendly meal, a verse:

Buddha Dharma is everywhere in all places
You may seek it everywhere, but it cannot be sought
Drumming on his belly in front of the dais:
    a ready-made phrase
The herdboy does indeed know how to ride the ox
    sitting backwards

NOTES

"Drumming his belly" feeling the satisfaction that transcendent wisdom brings.

"Riding the ox sitting backwards" Effortlessly riding the giant "ox" of the totality, the Zen adept out of compassion faces "backwards" into the world of relativity, the home of the unenlightened.

10: Zen Travels   (To attendant Huan)

The old man of Elephant Bone Mountain [Xuefeng] said, "When I left Lingnan, I was thirty-two years old. When I entered Min, I was already over forty." Let us investigate [what Xuefeng did during] this interval of over ten years. He received formal ordination in northeast

China and travelled around to all the Zen assemblies there. He went three times [to Mt. Touzi] and nine times climbed [Mt. Deshan]. He learned the truth of form and emptiness from a saying of Yanguan's. Together with Mr. Hui and Mr. Sui, he was a personal attendant of Deshan for a long time. [At a certain point] he lamented that he had never gotten to see Shandong [and set out to travel there]. Midway there, the straw hat he was wearing dropped into the water, but he went on without paying any attention.

I have never heard of [a case of a sincere student of the Dharma] staying in one corner. So we know that [the story in the Huayan Sutra of Sudhana] going south, travelling through a hundred and ten towns, and studying with fifty-three enlightened teachers does not deceive us: [it was communicated] to impart a standard to later day students.

But what can be done? We are not far from the [Zen] ancients, but the style and standards of Zen are in serious decline.

Though you say you are visiting the south, in reality the substance [of a journey for knowledge] is not there. This is truly a cause for sadness. Your feeling is that "green mountains are easy to find, but enlightened teachers are hard to meet." You are abandoning one precious mountain [here] without climbing it, so where else will you go?

Go, go! Don't get stuck here. "Empty-handed you went, and empty-handed you return." You better wait with this saying to wash out your ears.

11: Will   (To Zen man Deqing)

If you study the Path as you did at first, then you will achieve the Path with plenty to spare. If you are scrupulous at the beginning but slack off at the end, the early achievements are lost.

I heard that when Wuzhun of Jingshan was [a monk] in the congregation, he once asked for instruction from our master Yanshi. The teacher told him, "There is no other strength to my study of the Path: I just don't let my will get spoiled."

All those who study the Path are like this, not only our late master Yanshi. If you put your body among the rivers and lakes, your unspoiled will should become more intense the longer you go on. If you return home after a journey of several decades, none of us will be able to know your unspoiled will.

Zen man Deqing of Tianpeng has been at here in this difficult place for a long time, making his mind imperturbable. He has come to me to seek a word to aid him in accomplishing the Path.

In the old days Yantou, in order to prompt the development of the true bodhisattva eye in new students, would break open the skin of his face and show one gaping eye.

Once you have seen it, it's not a matter of words. If you have not yet seen it, right now at a site on Shuang-Jing there is a teacher sitting in a great bodhimandala wearing a shirt of many colors beating a poison-smeared drum to show its form. You should go and look at it.

NOTES

"Bodhisattva" An enlightening being: an enlightened person who functions in the world to help others to awaken. To be a bodhisattva was the aim of Great Vehicle Buddhism in general and of the Zen school.

"Bodhimandala" A site of enlightenment; an array of enlightening beings illustrating the process of the teaching of enlightenment.

"Poison-smeared drum" See #4.

12: The Inexhaustible Treasury
(To Shao Lu, chief of instruction at Nanquan Temple)

This Dharma-gate of ours is called the inexhaustible treasury, the gate of merit and wisdom and supernatural powers, the most special of the special, the most excellent of the excellent. It is likened to a great mass of jewels: all the gems most prized by the world are there: garlands of pearls, ivory, jade. There is a Great Chief, standing upright in the middle: to those who come from all directions seeking jewels, he gives them freely.

In a snap of the fingers, he has gone through hundreds and thousands and ten of thousands and hundreds of millions of eons. No one knows how many have come [to him] empty and returned full. He is called the Chief of Great Riches: he is the Tathagata.

Anyone whose root capacity is bold and sharp will ascend directly to the precious abode without passing through the cities of illusion. The reason for [the enlightened] staying temporarily in the cities of illusion is to uphold correct perception and protect correct mindfulness [there]. Using nothing but a straightforward, genuine mind without falsity, they traverse the realms of dreamlike illusion and true reality. Seeking to have awareness without craving, they apply themselves tirelessly. When they meet [reality] face to face, they rub their palms together and laugh. They naturally mesh with the groove wherever they are and suit the potentials [of the audience/situation] in everything they say. They turn the wheel of the True Dharma and manifest the land of the Jewel King.

This is the business of teaching. If we push open further toward transcendence, we discover the True Light. Here, if we comprehend what our original face was before our fathers and mothers were born, not only worldly jewels, but also the world-transcending ones, are all here in this.

The Buddha said to [his companion] Ananda, "When you carry the begging bowl now, you should follow the form of the Seven Buddhas [of Antiquity]." Ananda asked, "What is the form of the Seven Buddhas?" The World Honored One called to Ananda and Ananda answered, "Yes?" The World Honored One said, "Take the bowl and go."

Ah! The assembly on Spirit Peak is still in session a thousand years later.

You may bow your head at these words, but I still will not approve.

Shao Lu, the chief of the temple, is going to Quannan to pay a visit on a patron with whom he has links. He will return with yellow-faced old Gautama to do great buddha-deeds. I write this to give him food for his journey. As for so-called "sayings that match the potential", it's all up to you, Shao Lu. Come back loaded full, and I'll explain for you and break it up.

NOTES

"Tathagata" An epithet of the Buddha, meaning "the one who has come from Thusness," the one who appears from within the totality of reality-as-it-is to express the teachings that enable people to open up their enlightened perception.

"The World Honored One" Another epithet of the Buddha.

"The Seven Buddhas" In Zen lore, ancient buddhas who proceeded the historical buddha, propounding the Dharma in earlier ages.

"The assembly on Spirit Peak" where the Buddha Shakyamuni started the Zen transmission, communicating the wordless gist of his teachings by holding up a flower.

"Gautama" The historical buddha, the Indian prince Siddharta who left home and family to seek enlightenment; who found transcendent wisdom and went forth to disseminate it in the world of classical India; also known as Shakyamuni, the sage of the Shakya clan.

13: The Lineage of Zen

In the gate of Shaolin, the rarest, most excellent beings have been fierce and determined and beyond measure, possessing the unique eye to transcend the [then current formulation of] the school and its guiding principles. Only thus could they be fit to take on the responsibility [of propagating the Dharma]. Definitely unqualified are those with petty knowledge and petty virture, with disdainful arrogant attitudes, who take a step forward but then take a step back.

Observe Huike, the Second Patriarch: what a model he was! He stood in the snow and cut off his arm, but was unable to enter [enlightenment]. But when [under Bodhidharma's prodding] he searched for mind and there was no mind, all entanglements abruptly ceased. "When an eighty-year-old man comes on stage, how could it be child's play?"

Through eight transmissions, it came to [Mazu] in Jiangxi. Eleven more generations, and it came to Dongshan. With Mazu it was "whole potential, whole function", renovating and changing and opening up a road through. With Dongshan it was "the words of Lu and the songs of Ba" [harking back to the ancients], turning back again to a groove that had been lost.

These two elders were both from Sichuan. Dongshan also found a young man [who was a worthy successor, namely Wuzu]. Father and son, double dark and double light, they netted sixty or seventy percent of the outstanding people in the China: among them people like Miyin, Wenshu, Fohai. Yuanwu first called on Hao of Yuquan: both of them were local products of the Sichuan basin. Powerful people to bear the responsibility [of the Dharma] [have appeared there] continuously up to the present: the whole world knows of them.

Some have come along later who have heard of the reputation [of these great teachers], but who do not seek their Path. Though they come from the same area, they stay with what is familiar to them. If you act like this and claim to be in the Zen school, I won't be a part of it.

Zen man Hai has suddenly announced he is returning home because his [first] teacher is getting old [and needs to be cared for]. I give him these instructions:

In the old days, the Ancient Spirit rubbed him on the back, and the Ancient Buddha emitted light. If you do not teach with the style of [Mazu's greatest disciple] Baizhang, then it will not be enough to repay the benevolence and virtue of your teacher. Ponder this and work hard on it.

As for what was said about the unique eye to transcend the [current embodiment] of the Zen school and its principles, wait until the glass river flows upstream, then come back and I'll explain it for you.

14: Why Wait?   (To Zen man Ying)

Zen man Ying of Tianpeng is departing from North Mountain at Jinling to go to North Mountain at Wulin. He came here to me to say goodbye. As soon as he opened his mouth I divined a verse and presented it to him:

> Once by mistake I drank the cold spring's water
> The bitter poison cut through my heart: I've grown old
>   without ever forgetting it
> Today is no comparison to former days
> We should probe to see if [the spring] is deep or shallow,
>   but we should not taste it

Zen man Ying did not accept this, and requested another turning word to serve as his companion in the Path while he did his meditation work. So [this is what I told him:]

The earlier generations furnish many examples of incurring defeat in the process of studying Zen and doing meditation work. You have heard them again and again, to the point that they have been spoiled [for you] through becoming overly familiar. You do not in the least consider them urgent or important. Now I am adding more mud on top of the dirt. If you find those examples or this example to be without benefit, you must go forward on your own, Zen man, and not retreat.

So again, I'll cite a case for you. Ascetic Bei [Xuansha] had a saying: "Bodhidharma did not come to China, the Second Patriarch did not go to India." If your eyes and brain are at all lively, you will not offend against the wind and waves: one look, and you see. Then the multiple confusion within your breast is spontaneously cleansed away without waiting to be swept out.

Just be able to apply your spiritual energy with bold lucidity. At all times, in all places, let go but don't let [this energy] be cut off. If the delusion that's been there of itself for such a long time is cut off for a moment, then you fall into emptiness, to haunt the fields and forests. As it is said, "If you are temporarily absent, you are like a dead person."

Why wait till the last day of your life?

If you think it is not so, ask the mountain peaks. They will surely check it out thoroughly for you.

When this talk was done, it was recorded and presented to Zen man Ying.

NOTES

"The cold spring's water, the bitter poison" The Buddhist teaching on emptiness, which is fatal to the ignorance, craving and aggression of the worldly self.

"Why wait till the last day of your life?" Enlightenment means the death of the false self, the self of delusion and conditioned perceptions: "dying the great death" before one's physical demise.

15: Ready-Made Samadhi   (To attendant De)

Zen man De, attendant to Huiri of Beijian, travelled to Jinling to visit me at Pure Stream Monastery. We talked about this and that: everything was ready-made samadhi. He had just come from the forge of an adept: a true embodiment of the saying "Dragons produce dragon cubs, phoenixes produce phoenix chicks."

When he was about to depart, he said to me, "Not even one word [of instruction]?" I told him, "The two words 'ready-made'—neutral, spontaneously so. As soon as you know it, you add a head on top of a head. But not knowing it is cutting off your head to seek to live. Even more [useless] it would be to add detailed verbal prescriptions to follow.

"Go, go, but do not divulge these words. If old man Beijian finds out he will scold you and say I still should be ignored. If you cannot hold firm any more, you better get to work yourself on the business of meditating. You should live up to what the meditation seat is for.

"I'll give another verse, to make the old man smile:

> You just took a slow walk by the bank of Beijian
>   ['North Bank']
> Now you move again to the river's edge at Stone River
>   ['Stone River']
> Most excellent, o son born of dragons and phoenixes!
> Why does the imperative of Nanyang have to be brand
>   new? hebi hanyang ling zhanxin

NOTES

"Dragons and phoenixes" represent the enlightened.

"Adding a head on top of a head" With direct experience, the added awareness of registering the experience ("I know I know") is superfluous.

"Cutting off the head to seek life" With direct experience, attempting to cut off registering the experience (I don't know I know) is needless, and self-defeating.

16: The Village of Dreams   (To Yuan shangren)

For patchrobed monks, with what's above them and below them, with this side and That Side, it's like fire burning ice: it does not leave traces. It is also their ordinary conduct.

Both longtime learners and new students enter this gate with their bodies in a village of dreams, trying to accomplish things in dreams, listening to people's sleeptalk. They may talk to themselves a lot and think they are awake. They nod their heads and agree with themselves, firmly refusing to believe that this eye-opening liberation exists. Our ancestral teacher Sengcan said, "If the eye is not asleep, all dreams are automatically removed. If the mind does not deviate, the myriad things are one suchness." How could he have been fooling us?

Mr. Yuan came here over a year ago. Every time he enters my room, I just cite for him the saying "[What is Buddha?] The cypress tree in the garden." I have never been easy with him: I have tried to make him reach insight at one point. If I always got my tongue cut off by him, I wouldn't be able to cope with him anymore.

> The frosty wind blows on my face
> Longing for the sun is quite human
> Suddenly I think of moving my bench
> I fully understand it's a leftover dream

So I wrote this and gave it to Mr. Yuan saying, "If Shuang-Jing Mountain did not still show the drum, I would not be able to give upside-down judgments for you."

NOTES

"This side" the ordinary world of relative reality.

"That Side" the realm of absolute reality.

"One Suchness" the fusion of the relative and the absolute: reality-as-it-is, embracing all particulars and the underlying unity.

"The drum" The Buddhist Teaching is likened to a drum, signalling the deluded to awaken. All phenomena, even the mountains, expound the Teaching.

17: The Transmission of Zen
(To Gui, the monk in charge of guests)

"The triple world is in confusion, the six planes of existence are dark and turbulent. Knowing mind and reaching the root, we are called shramanas." Once Buddha heard these words [from a monk, when he first ventured beyond the palace], he abandoned the wealth and honor of being ruler over a great kingdom, left the palace compound, left his family, and went into the mountains. For twelve years altogether he endured hunger and cold. His sole motive was to consummate this Path. "Eighty-year-olds dance only in order to teach their descendants."

At the end, Buddha held up a flower, and entrusted the treasury of the correct Dharma eye [to Kashyapa]. It was passed down from person to person through twenty-eight generations. The great teacher Bodhidharma was the youngest son of a king. He left his homeland and journeyed thousands of miles across the ocean to come here looking for people with the capacity for the Great Vehicle. He had no other motive but to transmit this Path.

After [Bodhidharma's] one flower opened into five petals, his descendants came to fill the world, and have done so continuously up until today. Among them there have been many great elders who abandoned upperclass status and wealth to enter this gate and live [very austere lives], eating and drinking only enough to keep alive, and [meditating all night] without ever lying down. Their stories are recorded in biography collections arranged so you can look them up. This was done just so you would study this Path, illuminate your true self, and escape from the cycle of birth and death.

People with will, having already uncovered it, must seek to follow the example of the former generations of elders. They must generate the great mind [intent on enlightenment]. They must take up the sword of wisdom, and with a single stroke, cut through the net of sentimental love and affection. They should seek out enlightened teachers, and stay with them until they are aroused to develop [the mind of enlightenment]. At all times they must apply their spiritual energy. It is like handling a crossbow: if you take careful aim before you shoot, naturally you won't miss one shot in ten thousand.

This is what is called "Standing on the summit of the highest peak, walking on the bottom of the deepest ocean." Turn back your steps to before you were an embryo in the womb, and focus your eyes on the locus of the subjective experience you construct in your daily activities: [it is like] snow flying in a redhot furnace, like ice hidden in a blazing fire. After a long long time, you are bound to have realization.

I met Gui, the monk in charge of guests, at Duxiu Peak. He was very interested in studying with me, but since the right time had not yet arrived, he could not yet dissipate his sentiments of doubt. I said to him, "Today I guarantee to you that this work [of sincerely seeking enlightenment] is never in vain."

NOTES

"The triple world" The world perceived through the lens of desire, the world as neutral form, and the formless realms experienced in meditation.

"The six planes of existence" Sentient beings cycle through six planes of existence: as ignorant animals, as suffering hell-beings, as greedy hungry ghosts, as jealous demigods, as self-controlled human beings, as gods in the heavens of desire.

"Eighty-year-olds dance only in order to teach their descendants" Shakyamuni Buddha was an embodiment of the timeless Dharmakaya, the body of reality of all the buddhas; his apparent search for enlightenment through leaving home and practicing austerities was undertaken to provide a lesson to the unenlightened.

"One flower opened into five petals" The five petals represent the "Five Houses" of Zen, the most influential Zen lineages in 9th and 10th century China.

18: Stopping   (To Xiu, an advanced student)

I returned to the south only when I was thirty. I heard a saying of Kongsou's: "For thirty years I travelled on foot: this affair means stopping." When I first encountered this saying, my mind was very uneasy. I was passing between the desks of two learned monks and saw [in an open text] some words by Qionggu quoting Yunmen:

"In the silent shining of the light is the place to stop and moor your boat."

Then I came to Teacup Peak. Within a few weeks, like the rest of the monks, I entered the abbot's room, where my late teacher quoted this to me: "Bodhidharma is buried at Bear Ear Mountain: why did he return to the West with one shoe?" I replied with "One drop of water, and the ink forms dragons in two places."

A day later, the dragon's sleeves were brushed open, and the whole face was revealed.

Subsequently, I gathered in my sense-faculties for four years [focusing on the inner light, rather than the external world]. After that, wherever I went I approached spiritual teachers and tasted the sweet and the bitter. In my movements and actions I never turned toward [enlightenment] or turned away from it.

Now it has been another thirty years. I have never been able to take it, to try to put on the look [of a Zen master]. Know for sure that this business [of enlightenment] is most definitely not to be taken casually. The word "stopping" is truly our one and only enlightened teacher.

Mr. Xiu is by natural endowment very pure and refined. He was two years in Xicheng, devoid of companions in the Path. I am happy to learn that Shitian, the elder of South Mountain, has moved to North Mountain. I said to Mr. Xiu, "Green mountains are easy to find, but enlightened teachers are hard to meet. This is precisely the time to dig under your robe [and find your true identity]."

Thus have I written so many ugly, clumsy phrases. The only reason has been to give Mr. Xiu a sense of urgency, so that he may make enlightenment his goal. Otherwise, he will sit in the bag of unconcern, and thirty years from now, no one will snap a finger [to wake him up]. Wouldn't that be too bad?

NOTES

"I travelled on foot" It was customary for students of Zen to travel around to the various Zen centers seeking contacts with enlightened teachers.

"Stopping" Stopping delusion, stopping false consciousness.

19: Centered

Within the ground covered by this sitting mat, there are no royal taxes, no exactions, no forced labor. The mind-tree is already harmonized and centered. If you to have the matching half of the split token, it is handed over at once. Once you arrive on That Side, who will be your neighbor?

NOTES

"The matching half of the split token" The metaphor is drawn from a means of verifying identities used in old China: a token would be split in half, one part given to the messenger, the matching part retained by the sender. When the returning messenger presented the other matching half, it would prove he was genuine. Prepared by the work of purification and meditative concentration, the learner's mind meshes with the Buddha-mind like the corresponding part of the token.

"That Side" see # 16.

20: Before and After

Up in the teaching hall, Stone River said:
"Before the day of enlightenment, you meet *Him* everywhere. When I ask, why do you say you do not know?
"After the day of enlightenment, every beat is the imperative. When I ask, why do you say you do not understand?
"On the day of enlightenment, dragons and snakes are easy to distinguish, patchrobed ones are hard to deceive.
Stone River held up his fist and said, "What is in my hand? You better study it."

NOTES

Him Dharmakaya Buddha, reality itself.

"The imperative" The pattern of cause and effect according to which the Buddhist Teaching must be carried out.

"Dragons and snakes" The enlightened and the unenlightened.

21: Today and Forever

Last night at midnight, Manjushri and Samantabhadra were both in front of the Good Dharma Hall. One said, "Today the Greatly Awakened World Honored One achieves true enlightenment." One said, "The World Honored One achieved true enlightenment endless eons ago."

Since these two could not decide, they were each given twenty blows of the staff by me and driven away at once. Nevertheless, officially we don't let in a needle [but unofficially a horse and cart can go through].

There was someone who asked Zhaozhou, "Who would you have take the beating?" Ha! He just knew how to ask about the fault, he did not know the correct imperative was already being carried out.

NOTES

Manjushri, the bodhisattva representing transcendental wisdom.

Samantabhadra, the bodhisattva whose name means "Universally Good", representing the universal teaching of enlightenment by all different means.

"The World Honored One" is Shakyamuni Buddha. See #12.

"Officially we don't let in a needle but unofficially a horse and cart can get through" In essence the Dharma is indescribable, but in practice all sorts of expedient means are used to express it.

22: On the anniversary of the death of his teacher

Stone River said:

"The first impulse, the last word, with standards, without guidelines. How can we take it up wrongly, how can we pass in on wrongly?"

Stone River held up the incense and said:

"If you say there was passing it on, you have wronged our former teacher. If you say there was no passing it on, you have also wronged our former teacher. Is there anyone who can speak?"

Stone River stuck the incense [into brazier] and said:

"How sad and desolate, today's brazier of incense. Even a heart made of iron is broken."

23: The Teacher's Method

Wuzu said, "To be an enlightened teacher means to drive off the ploughman's ox and snatch away the hungry man's food. He drives off the ploughman's ox to enable his seedling crops to grow. He snatches away the hungry man's food so he will never starve again."

Master Song-yuan said, "Even though you are forced to the brink of a ten thousand fathom precipice, it must be you yourself who consents to let go of your body and your life. If we drive off the ploughman's ox, how will the seedling crops grow? If we snatch away the hungry man's food, how will he never starve?"

Stone Rive commented: "When Song-yuan spoke like this, it seems that his plans were played out and his strength was exhausted. He made us all into doctors for dead horses. Little did he know that after the rain disperses in the eternal sky, the single expanse of wind and light belongs to each person."

NOTES

"The ploughman's ox" The ordinary person's mode of perceiving the world, based on conditioned judgments and desires, which blocks off enlightened perception.

"The hungry man's food" The mundane satisfactions sought by the ordinary person on the basis on the basis of conditioned judgments and desires.

"The single expanse of wind and light" Reality as a whole, which can be perceived by all people who activate their innate enlightened perception.

24: The Family Style

My family-style at Tiger Hill: inside empty, outside empty, 100% poor and destitute, sometimes raising a sound to stop an echo, sometimes pretending to be deaf and dumb. This is still commonplace small liberation: but what is great liberation?

[a long silence]

No three listeners have the same opinion.

25: A visit from an old friend

On the occasion of a visit by master of the canon Yungu, Stone River went up to the teaching hall and said:

"Forty years ago, I received a new thing. Now a companion in the Path comes visiting, and all I can do is bring it out. But tell me, what thing is this?

"Over the bluegreen mountain outside the gate, the white clouds fly. The willows by the mountain stream invite the traveller to return. No wonder after he sits down I keep urging him to take a drink. Since we parted, it has been rare to meet such a profound person, alas!"

26: Beyond Affirmation and Denial

Among those living the monastic life, those who are busy and noisy do not know quiet and emptiness, and those who are quiet and empty do not know bustle and noise. With stillness and noise both forgotten, where affirmation and negation do not reach, try to say something for us to see [the extent of your insight].

27: Putting a roof on the Dharma-hall

Great compassion is the room. The emptiness of all phenomena is the seat. The buddhas of past present and future, along with all the beings of the whole universe, dwell together in this room, and sit together on this seat. Each and every one of them is working on the fundamental business and turning the wheel of the Great Dharma.

But what about when Yuquan looked up to count the corners of the houses, and Deshan turned his back and put on straw sandals? Already old, it's hard to bear a windy, rainy evening: we take a scrap of tile to cover our heads.

28: See for Yourself

Up in the teaching hall, Stone River said:

"A thousand explanations, ten thousand explanations, are not as good as seeing it once in person face to face."

Stone River called to the assembly in a loud voice, and everyone lifted their heads. Then Stone River said:

"You have eyes but no ears: you are sitting by the fire in August."

NOTES

"Sitting by the fire in August" Relying on a teacher to point out reality, ignoring one's own innate capacity for enlightened perception.

29: An Imperial Invitation

In the autumn of 1246, Stone River was invited to Lingyin Temple in Lin-an, the capital of the Southern Song dynasty.

He held up the imperial summons and said:

"Do all of you know [what this is]? Inside the golden palace [the Emperor] casually beckons with his hand, and even people at the stage of buddha nod their heads [obediently]. Today [this imperial order] has come down into the hands of this inconsequential monk, inviting me to explain [the Dharma] thoroughly to everyone."

Stone River ascended to the teacher's seat, held up incense, and said:

"This incense is dedicated to our present august imperial majesty: may his sagely lifetime extend ten thousand years, ten thousand times ten thousand years!"

After answering questions, he said:

"This expanse of wind and light is nowhere absent. By means of it, heaven covers us and earth supports us and the sun and moon shine. Buddhas and enlightened teachers use it to spread compassion. True kings use it to extend their civilizing influence.

"Thus does our sage Son of Heaven unfurl his imperial policy on a wide scale and extend his fructifying benevolence everywhere. Even the abundance of the mountains and forest are among the recipients of his blessings.

"Through some mistake I have received the imperial benevolence [and have been appointed] to fill the empty seat at Lingyin Temple. I am ashamed of my decrepitude: I am scarcely fit for the responsibility. But I think of [my predecessors] uncle Xiatang and grandpa Song-yuan both moving forty years now. Now this inconsequential monk follows on their heels. Three generations [of our lineage] at one gate [Lingyin Temple]: how could such a conjuncture be fortuitous? In this life or another life, how can I repay [this benevolence]?"

Stone River raised the whisk and called to the assembly:

"I vow to transmit the Fourth Patriarch's untransmitted message, and to look up to and salute Nanshan's million billion springs."

Stone River also cited this case:

"Emperor Taizong asked a monk, 'Where have you come from?' The monk said, 'I was lying in a hermitage in the clouds at Lushan.' The Emperor said, 'Lying among the clouds in a remote place, you do not pay court to heaven: why did you come here?' The monk said nothing. [Zen master] Xuedou supplied an answer for him: 'It is impossible to escape [Your Majesty's] perfect civilizing influence.'

"For the new abbot of Lingyin, happiness is hard to meet, but I will turn another phrase. [If Emperor Taizong had asked me]: 'Lying among the clouds in a remote place, you do not pay court to heaven: why did you come here?' I would just report: 'Today I am serving in person the Heavenly Visage.'"

Then Stone River left the teacher's seat.

NOTES

Emperor Taizong brother of the founder of the Song dynasty, reigned 976-997.

"Son of Heaven" epithet of the Chinese emperor, seen as the mediator between Heaven and human society.

30: Stone River's Farewell to the Assembly at Tiger Hill

"An imperial summons has come down from the nine-layered heavens: the luster of the precious ink is still fresh. They are moving a dead tree from the cliff to transplant it on Vulture Peak.

"You must realize that [true] mind itself has no [false states of] mind: it does not follow the ruts 'going' and 'coming'. Objects themselves are not objects [as falsely perceived]: they are not shaped in the outlines of 'this' and 'that'. The holy peaks join hands and turn back together. The various teaching centers talk with each other shoulder to shoulder. At just such a time, can we apply the word 'parting' or not?"

Stone River slapped the meditation bench and said:

"Farewell, cloudy mountain: I'll think of you fondly."

NOTES

"Vulture Peak" The site of many of Buddha's famous teaching assemblies: used here as a metaphor for Lingyin Temple, which was at the top of the Southern Song system of officially recognized Zen temples.

31: Entry into Lingyin Zen Temple

As he entered the temple, Stone River pointed to the temple gate and said:

"Putting to rest all outside entanglements, there is no road for mental constructs. Entering the gateless gate, three steps more than in former days."

He gave a shout and said:

"The spirit tracks are not where the monkey howls."

At the buddha-shrine, Stone River pointed with the incense to the buddha-image and said:

"This old guy has faults that reach to heaven. He has never stopped dragging in ordinary people. Although we do not enter your shrine, we repay injustice with injustice. But how can we let you go?"

Stone River held up the imperial summons and said:

"The jewel in [Buddha's] topknot?—this is it. It is like the udumbara flower that appears once in a long period."

He looked around and said:

"Do you want to know the truth? Cut off your conceptual faculty: only then will you be able to listen."

Stone River held up the robe of Song-yuan [his teacher's teacher] and said:

"In the Dayu Range, at Huangmei in the middle of the night, [the robe given to the Sixth Patriarch] could not be seized by force: when it was freely yielded, there was more than enough. Today's public case is ready-made, but inevitably we meet an error with an error."

He held up the robe and said:

"I dare to ask this robe: Passed on by Baiyun, handed down by
Song-yuan, what do you explain? The troublesome spring wind has
never stopped."

Then he put the robe over his shoulders.

[When he taught at Lingyin, Song-yuan had directed his robe to
be put in his stupa when he died, because no one in the assembly there
had understood him. Song-yuan prophesied that in thirty years his
grandson would come. Song-yuan's robe was given to Stone River
by keeper of the stupa Zongli.]

NOTES

"The spirit tracks are not where the monkey howls" The "monkey" represents
the discriminating intellect of the unenlightened.

"The robe could not be seized by force" When the Fifth Patriarch of Zen
recognized the humble workman Huineng as his successor, many of his
disciples were outraged. Some pursued Huineng after he left the Fifth Patriarch's
place at Huangmei, intending to take back the robe that was symbolic of his
successorship. But when they overtook Huineng in the Dayu Range, he threw
down the robe for them to take, but magically, they could not lift it.

"We meet an error with an error" Any particular presentation of the Buddhist
Teaching is necessarily incomplete and only provisionally "true", and in this
sense, an "error": an error used to deal with the error of deluded conventional
existence.

"The troublesome spring wind" The spring wind represents the message
of the Buddhist Teaching; it is "troublesome" because of the ultimate challenge
it poses to the conventional self.

"He put the robe over his shoulders" symbolizing that he was the true successor
of Song-yuan.

32: A Challenge

After offering incense to the Emperor, the high ministers of
state, and to all the lords and officials present, and to his teacher Yanshi,
Stone River said:

"Do all of you want to recognize the jewel of the Dharma King?"

He struck a blow to his left with the whisk and said: "This is it."

"Do all of you want to recognize the jewel of the [worldly] King?"

He struck a blow to his right with the whisk and said: "This is it."

"Those whose spirits are sharp will see immediately, and then they will realize that the jewel of the Dharma King is the jewel of the worldly King and the jewel of the worldly king is the jewel of the Dharma king.

"This is why my teacher's teacher Song-yuan carried this jewel from Tiger Hill and climbed this mountain looking for these people to hand it over to with both hands. Thirty years later it has become an unfinished case. I too have come from Tiger Hill, and I have been given the Dharma-robe as a token of credibility. It being so, I cannot avoid finishing the case for him."

Stone River held up the whisk and said:

"Functioning with [false states of] mind is bound to go wrong. Seeking without [true] intent likewise."

He also cited this:

"There was a monk who saw Emperor Taizong of our own [Song] dynasty at court and said, 'Do you remember me, Your Majesty?' The Emperor said, 'Where did we meet?' The monk said, 'We parted on Spirit Peak [where Buddha preached, and have not seen each other again] until right now.' The Emperor said, 'What is your proof?' The monk said nothing."

Stone River said:

"Taizong hung the heavenly mirror up on high, and met the situation with a thrust of his own. This monk was thunder sounding out of a silent abyss: what he offered was real. Even so, he could not cut off the tongues of everyone in the world.

"Today an inconsequential monk borrows water and makes offerings of flowers. We parted on Spirit Peak [and meet again now]: what is the proof?"

Stone River stood up, bowed from the waist, then put his hands on his hips and said:

"Today we respectfully wish for ten thousand years of life for His Majesty's sagely existence."

NOTES

"Held up his whisk" Zen masters held up the whisk to symbolize their mastery of the Buddha Dharma, the teaching of enlightenment, of which they were living representatives.

"Cut off the tongues of everyone in the world" Display mastery so convincing as to silence every doubt.

33: Forming Associations

At a small night gathering Stone River said:

"Mind like the realm of emptiness shows the Dharma equal to emptiness. When witnessing emptiness, there is no phenomena of affirmation or denial.

"Why then this saying? 'In ancient times forming associations was like refining gold: after a hundred smeltings, its color did not change. Nowadays forming associations is like a violent flow suddenly kicking up dust and dirt.'

"[In saying this] the great master 'Zen Moon' only saw that the point of the awl is sharp, he did not see that the chisel head is square.

"Last spring I parted with all of you: today we meet again. One could say that the one assembly on Spirit Peak is still in session. If not for behavior like pines in the cold, if not for associations like pure gold that does not change color, how could this be?

"Surely you have seen [this story]: Linji said to his assembly, 'I want to establish the message of the school of [my teacher] Huangbo. Who will become my successor?' At the time Puhua and Kefu came forward to ask about his health, then left. The next day they asked Linji, 'What were you saying yesterday, Master?" Linji immediately struck them, and the two men bowed in homage.

"A-li-li! Linji founding a school this way, the two men becoming successors this way—how far off it is! I have no Dharma that can be founded, but I want all of you to become successors. But tell me, become successors to what? Where is it warm in November?"

Stone River also cited this story:

"When Yangqi was studying with Ciming the second time, he asked, 'How is it when the bird in the dark ravine is murmuring, saying goodbye to the clouds and entering the chaotic peaks?' Ciming said: 'I am walking in the wild weeds, you are entering a remote village.' Yangqi said, 'Officially, not a needle is let in, but let me ask another question.' Ciming immediately shouted. Yangqi said, 'Good shout.' Ciming shouted again. Yanqi shouted too. Ciming gave two shouts one after another. Yanqi then bowed in homage."

Stone River commented:

"One man sits astride a three-legged donkey. One man rides a three-horned tiger. In a village of three families they stand shoulder to shoulder. On a cliff ten thousand fathoms high, they take a step forward. Two buckets of black ignorance rubbing together. What can be done? Both committed the fall of words. Ha!"

NOTES

"The point of the awl is sharp, the chisel head is square" Ideally, when people come together to study Zen, worldly motivations should be absent; in the event, worldly motivations can only be cleared away little by little.

"The assembly on Spirit Peak" where Buddha initiated the Zen transmission.

"Like pines in the cold" Upright, aloof, ever fresh.

"Where is it warm in November?" Where does the True Teaching still flourish this late in Buddhist history?

"The fall of words" Making Zen dialogue into an exercise of conceptual-verbal ingenuity.

34: Accept your lot

Up in the hall Stone River said:

"Last night at midnight Manjushri was riding Mount Wutai and Samantabhadra was riding Mount Emei: they ascended [the holy mountains] Tiantai and Nanyue and met at the stupa where immortals are made.

"They are inside the eyes and ears of all of you people, talking about the length of the spoons in the east house and the size of the pots in the west house. It appears that all of you are acting foolish, and do not perceive them at all. As usual, you are scattering yourselves."

Suddenly Stone River picked up the staff and brandished it and said:

"Aware that with the passing years your bodies will age, each of you should accept your lot peacefully and thus pass the remainder of your lives."

NOTES

Manjushri and Samantabhadra See notes to #21. According to Chinese Buddhist tradition, Mount Wutai was the abode of Manjushri and Mount Emei the abode of Samantabhadra.

"The length of the spoons and the size of the pots" The mundane affairs which preoccupy ordinary people and submerge their capacity for transcendence.

"Accept your lot" In Buddhist terms, the innate endowment and true identity of every person is the capacity for enlightened wisdom and compassion.

35: Bluegreen Mountain, White Clouds

Stone River cited this case:

"A monk asked Xuedou, 'What is the true master of Xuedou like?' Xuedou said, 'Why don't you ask the people on Mount Xuedou?' The monk said, 'Then he holds heaven and earth fast.' Xuedou said, 'You have left the gate, but I'm afraid you have not arrived yet. Who is it on the road that has been waiting forever for you to come?'"

Stone River commented:

"There was accuracy in the question, and the answer did not spurn the questioner's potential."

Stone River called to the great assembly and said:

"Do you see Xuedou? The bluegreen mountain is facing them, but few people recognize it. Instead they just look in vain to the white clouds rolling up and rolling out in the emptiness."

NOTES

"The bluegreen mountain" represents reality.

"The white clouds" represent delusion.

36: Lecturing on a sutra

On the *tian-ji* festival, Stone River went up to the teaching hall and said:

"An inconsequential monk, I ascend to this precious seat. Using empty space as a mouth, and the myriad forms as a tongue, I lecture on the Chapter on Lifespan of the Benevolent King [from the Benevolent King Sutra]. I am afraid the lecturing masters will hear of this and think I am infringing on their trade and stealing their business.

"But for now let me explain the title ['The lifespan of the Benevolent King']."

Stone River hit the meditation bench with the whisk and said:

> A snap of the fingers: Zen has no private tune
> All are sounds for a thousand autumns,
> 　　　for ten thousand years

NOTES

At the *Tian-ji* festival, the Buddhist community paid homage to the ruler.

The Benevolent King Sutra outlines a Buddhist view of just rulership. Buddha entrusts the secular rulers with the responsibility to act as protectors of the Dharma.

36: The Dharma on New Year's Day

On new year's day Stone River went up to the teaching hall and said:

"The Buddha Dharma at the start of the new year: Jingqing said it exists, Mingjiao said it doesn't. Both of them lost the advantage. You must go to the staff to decide."

Then Stone River held up the staff and said:

"The Buddha Dharma at the start of the new year: Does it exist? The staff does not answer. Does it not exist? The staff still does not answer. How is it when all at once existence and non-existence, new and old are taken away?"

Stone River brandished the staff and said:

"Making the rounds of the [Dharma] halls having [the monks] drink tea."

NOTES

"The start of the new year" in these sayings refers to the time before anything exists. If there were no world of delusion, would the teaching of enlightenment exist or not?

"The staff" is the symbol of the Zen masters' ability to teach.

"Drink tea" in order to wake up.

37: The Staff

Up in the teaching hall Stone River held the staff horizontal and called to the assembly:

"Isn't there anyone who can pass through here? [Even if you can, you get] three thousand blows in the morning, eight hundred blows in the evening. The hand turns back and forth and produces clouds and rain.

"If you cannot pass through, modern is not ancient and ancient is not modern. Try to leap up so we can see you."

Then Stone River brandished the staff.

NOTES

"Modern is not ancient, ancient is not modern" when students fail to reach the timeless standard of enlightenment set forth by the ancient masters.

38: The Dharma cannot be sought

At a vegetarian feast Stone River said:

"The Dharma cannot be explained, because it is beyond spoken language and written words. The Dharma cannot be sought, because it is apart from seeing and hearing, feeling and knowing.

"Last night the head monks of the two halls tried to explain what cannot be explained, and all of you tried to seek what cannot be sought. This being so, how can we dare refuse to make offerings: we should be spending ten thousand ounces of gold.

"When I talk like this, isn't there anyone who will tweak my nose?"

He answered himself:

"Who will dare?"

39: A Turning Word

At end of summer retreat Stone River said:

"The autumn wind fills our robes: the brethren are departing in various directions. I have a turning word that I will cite to see you off.

"Number one: do not hear it wrong. Number two: do not understand it wrong. Number three: when you meet people, do not quote it wrong. If you make no mistakes in these three, you have still slandered me. Isn't there anyone who can avoid this?"

Then he picked up the staff and brandished it once.

NOTES

"Summer retreat" Zen monks customarily left off travelling and gathered together in their monasteries and retreats for the three months of summer for a period of intensive meditation.

"A turning word" Zen sayings with multiple layers of meaning, intended to interact with and transform the mind of the student.

"You have still slandered me" The student who accepts any of the teacher's formulations as a final truth has misunderstood the real intent.

40: A Disciple's Gratitude and Resentment

On the anniversary of the death of Song-yuan, Stone River said:

"Before you see this old man, heaven is above and earth is below. After you see him, mountains are mountains and rivers are rivers. Fifty years since we parted: my whole body is gratitude and resentment. Leaving aside gratitude for now, what do I resent?

"Immeasurably great men cannot pick up their feet: they drag in their children and grandchildren. When will they stop disturbing the spring wind?"

NOTES

"Before you see" distinctions are seen as ultimately real.

"After you see" the oneness of the absolute does not contradict the multiplicity of the particulars.

"They drag in their children . . . disturbing the spring wind" Teachers present their students with the danger that the students may cling to the teachers' particular formulations of the truth, and be blocked off from the enlightening influence of reality itself ("the spring wind").

41: Always Secure

Sun and moon do not shine on it. Heaven and earth do not cover and support it. In the holocaust at the end of the age, this is always secure. When the myriad phenomena are obliterated, its whole body shows. It follows the currents without changing. Amidst noise and turmoil it is always still and calm.

The benevolent light of the One Path: who does not have a share in it? The ancients strung everything together with this: since they did this with things and events, what about inner truth? The ancients cannot fool me, and I cannot fool all of you. Say something where officially not even a needle is allowed in.

42: Break the Golden Chains

How about it? What is it? The lion is in the gate. The tiger is on the seat. Out of a thousand or ten thousand people, one or a half [will see]. In the light of sparks struck from stone or a bolt of lightning, break open the golden chains. If you hesitate in thought, as always, you have stumbled by and missed it.

NOTES

"The golden chains" of mystical rapture in which a dualistic sense of self/other, experiencing subject/experienced state is still present.

43: This Dharma

At a wintertime vegetarian feast Stone River cited this story:

"Bodhisattva Vasubandhu ascended into a palace in the Tushita Heaven and visited Maitreya: there he listened to an exposition of the Dharma. [Back on earth] three years went by. [His brother] Asanga asked him [after he returned], 'What Dharma did Maitreya preach?' Vasubandhu said, 'He just spoke of this Dharma, but his holy voice was so pure and elegant it made people happy to listen.'

Stone River said:

"They look similar, but they're not the same. What you worthy monks were talking about last night: wasn't it this Dharma? When the temple supervisor arranges for offerings, isn't it this Dharma?

"If someone were suddenly to ask, 'What is this Dharma?' just tell him, 'In the [tiny] pores of the lotus root, riding a giant roc [as it soars on high], causally pulling down the moon from the sky.'"

NOTES

Maitreya is the Future Buddha, who dwells in Tushita Heaven until the time when he will come down to be born on earth and usher in an era of peace and prosperity.

Vasubandhu and Asanga were two great Indian Buddhist philosophers, reckoned among the patriarchs of Zen.

"This Dharma" the teaching of enlightenment as presented to the present age.

44: Smelted in a great furnace

On one occasion, the community of monks was casting a large communal pot. Up in the teaching hall Stone River said:

"If we discuss this affair [of enlightenment], it is like smelting metal in a great furnace, fanning up a fierce fire, working it and refining it ten thousand times, getting rid of all the slag, until it is nothing but unmixed pure metal. Only then is it put into the mold and cast into a great vessel.

"Surely you have read how Baizhang on his second visit to Mazu received a thunderous shout and was deaf for three days, how Huangbo heard of this and unconsciously stuck his tongue out [in awe]. How can we not call this getting cast in a great furnace? But if we do call it getting cast in a great furnace, then we are pressing down a free man and making him a slave [downgrading the students' own effort]. Right now, isn't there anyone here who has not been melted and forged?"

Then Stone River gave a shout and got up and left.

45: Who can sing an answering refrain?

Up in the teaching hall Stone River said:

"Yunmen's one tune: on the twenty-fifth day of the last month, it startles the iron ox of Jiazhou and knocks down the horned tiger of Shishuang. Since the time is fitting, the causes and conditions can hardly be coarse and crude. Isn't there anyone here who can sing an answering refrain?"

Stone River held up the whisk and said:

"I will go on chanting and singing by myself."

Then he tapped the meditation bench with the whisk and got up and left.

Yunmen [d. 949] was one of the all-time greats of the Zen school.

"The iron ox of Jiazhou, the horned tiger of Shishuang" Two colossal statues, used here to represent the presumed solidity of the phenomenal world.

46: Ancient and Modern

What the ancients used, the moderns use. What the moderns do, the ancients did.

There's just one place that's obscure. It is not that the Sichuan monk holds the snake still between his teeth and the Zhejiang monk beats it. So I ask you, where is the place that's obscure and hard to understand: is it on the part of the ancients or the part of the moderns?

Meeting without words, feelings and intentions are enought. Do not be sad after we part: meetings with profound people are rare.

NOTES

Sichuan and Zhejiang are regions at opposite ends of China.

47: How can we escape?

Stone River cited this case:

"A monk asked Dongshan, 'When cold and hot come, how can we escape?' Dongshan said, 'Why not go to where there is no cold and hot?' The monk asked, 'What is the place where there is no cold and hot?' Dongshan said, 'When it's cold the cold kills you and when it's hot the heat kills you.'"

Stone River commented:

"In Dongshan's school they have the five ranks of correct and biased interchanging and intercommunicating. The station of the correct is correct, yet still biased. The station of the biased is biased, yet still correct. Ultimately, what is the place where there is no cold and hot?"

Stone River gave a shout and said:

"Don't go to sleep!"

NOTES

"The five ranks" In this teaching device from the Cao-Dong stream of Zen, the seeker's progress is charted in terms of the relationship between the absolute truth realm ("the correct") and the realm of the relative ("the biased"). Here is one version, with comments by Dongshan's great disciple Caoshan:

1. The absolute within the relative (The level of the ordinary person, for whom the absolute is totally concealed within mundane conventional reality)
"The moon in the water, the image in the mirror: [since the absolute is] fundamentally without origin or extinction, how could any traces [of it] remain?"
2. The realtive within the absolute (The level of the meditator absorbed in the emptiness of all things)
"A piece of emptiness pervading everywhere, all senses silent."
3. Coming from within the absolute (The breakthrough of enlightenment)
"The whole body revealed, unique; the root source of all things; in it there is neither praise nor blame."
4. Arrive within the relative (The enlightened person's return to the world, which no longer obstructs him or her)
"Going along with things and beings without hindrance; a wooden boat empty inside, getting through freely by being empty."
5. Arrival in both at once (The stage of complete mastery; being on both sides at once)
"The absolute is not necessarily void, the relative is not necessarily actual; there is neither turning away nor turning towards."
See T. Cleary, *Timeless Spring*, p. 51.

48: Still Lacking

Stone River cited this case:
"Gentleman in Waiting Wang visited Linji. They were together in front of the monks' hall. Wang said, 'Do the monks of this hall read the scriptures?" Linji said, 'They do not read the scriptures.' Wang said, 'Do they sit in meditation?' Linji said, 'They do not sit in meditation.' Wang said, 'What after all do you teach them to do?' Linji said, 'I teach them all to become enlightened Zen masters.' Wang said, 'Though golden flakes are precious, when they fall into the eye they block vision.' Linji said, 'I knew you were a conventional fellow.'"
Stone River commented:

"Inside the gate there are true gentlemen, outside the gate true gentlemen are arriving. Wang appeared in the body of a courtier to stimulate Linji. Though this business [of enlightenment] was not absent, when we check them out, they were still lacking one move. But say, was this lack on the part of Gentleman in Waiting Wang, or Linji? Those with eyes should try to check and see."

49: Buddha's Body

On the anniversary of Buddha's nirvana, Stone River said:

"[Buddha said,] 'If anyone tries to see me in terms of form or seek me by means of sound, this person is travelling a false path.' At the end of his life, he rubbed his breast and said to the assembly, 'Behold well my body, with its purple lustre and golden hue. Today it exists, tomorrow it will not.'

"This old guy revealed his shadow in two places, stretched out his body in one place. But say, is his former statement right, or is the latter statement right?"

50: The Net is Cast over You

Stone River held up the staff and showed it to the assembly and said:

"On Spirit Peak [Buddha] spread a net that covered heaven. Whether you can speak or you cannot speak, you are all within it.

"But what about the one who cannot be trapped, who cannot be called back?"

He brandished the staff and said:

"The net is cast over you."

NOTES

"The staff" See #36, note, and #37.

"Spirit Peak" where Buddha started the Zen transmission.

"The one who cannot be trapped" The real person, our buddha-nature.

51: Inside an Atom of Dust

Up in the teaching hall Stone River said:

"Before the double barrier is opened, wrapped around with hundred and thousands of layers. After the myriad doors are opened, piercing and penetrating in all dimensions. But how is it before the myriad doors open?"

After a long silence, he said:

"I knew the mountains and rivers were all obstructing you. Your comings and goings take place inside an atom of dust."

52: Abiding Nowhere

In the summer of 1250, Stone River was invited to take up the abbacy of Xingsheng Wanshou Zen Temple at Mount Jingshan near the capital Lin-an. He bade farewell to the congregation at Lingyin:

". . . It is the Emperor's command. Right now it is the height of the hot season, and the imperial emissary is pushing me to go. But I must take a short time to bid farewell to the Zen community here. Each of you must uphold and protect [the Dharma] well.

"There has never been any difference between joining and parting. There is no aspect of going or coming."

He also spoke a verse:

Tower in the clouds, moonlight palace, land of crystal
Abiding nowhere, dependent on nothing, a single Mind
Don't say there is meeting and parting
Another year when we meet again it will just be right now

53: Greetings to the Assembly at Jingshan

Stone River summoned the whole assembly and said:

"I have come from Lingyin up to this mountain, and have gotten to meet all of you. I have nothing at all: I just pick up a pitcher of east-west stream water and a few scraps of south-north mountain clouds. What's the need to deliberately match people's sentiments? I'll just tell you: don't be surprised if I take [everything] lightly. You have been standing a long time: [you can go now]."

54: A Thousand Mouths to Feed

Up in the teaching hall, Stone River told the assembled monks this:

"The great being Guanyin on her one body has 84,000 mudra-arms. Beautiful they are indeed, but if we made a shirt for her, where would we put so many sleeves?

"Is this as good as me here at Jingshan, with a multitude of tasks, putting forth a hand for each one, spontaneously taking care of all business? Nevertheless, a rich household thinks that having only a thousand mouths to feed is too few."

NOTES

Guanyin The bodhisattva representing compassion, depicted in East Asia as woman.

"Mudra" Finger positions used for meditative focus which in Buddhist iconography symbolize various aspects of the powers and activities of enlightening beings.

55: The Harvest

October 1st, good news: we store up the water and report the first clear sky. A new coolness arises in all directions. Grain fills the fields, urging the people to gather it in soon. Head by head, grain by grain, you must take loving care of it. Don't let it make a mess all over the ground. Wait until last year's and this year's public taxes and private rents are paid all at once in full: then nothing can stop you, once full, from forgetting a hundred times you were hungry, drumming your belly and singing songs and living out the rest of your days. But say, what song will you be singing? Happy and alive, happy and alive!

56: Do not pass the time in vain

December 15th: fallen leaves and piles of clouds, a cold wind pushing at the door. Under the bright window the most senior monk is walking east and west: all are places where he upholds his practice. People who study the mystery must remember the ancients' saying: 'A hundred years of time [is all you've got]: do not pass it in vain!'"

57: Grandpa Buddha

At the ceremony of washing the buddha-image Stone River said:

"Old grandpa Yellow Face: from the treasury of the realm of reality his body issued forth with correct essential knowledge. From correct essential knowledge he flowed forth with the knowledge attained after enlightenment, and from this he flowed forth with great compassion. From Tushita Heaven he came down to be born in India. He was like the rivers, like the mountains. He entered the sea of birth and death and went against the flow of birth and death. The Dharma was his citadel and compassion was his ferry.

"Completely awake, completely still, transcendent and free: half closed, half open, letting both go, gathering both in. [In the Zen school] Buddha has been called 'three pounds of hemp', 'a dry piece of shit', 'an old monk from India'. Some [said they] would break his shrine, some [said they] would strike him dead with one blow.

"It can rightly be said that his benevolence was so great it is impossible to repay. So many things have emerged despite everything because of it.

"Today on Buddha's birthday among us unworthy grandsons, a verse is spoken:

> Empty-handed, holding a hoe
> Going on foot, riding a water buffalo
> People are passing over the bridge
> The bridge is flowing, not the river
> Moving the earth, the pure wind keeps coming without a stop
> Bah!

NOTES

"Old Yellow Face" was a nickname for Buddha in the Zen school.

"The realm of reality" in Sanskrit, *Dharmadhatu.*

"Half closed, half open" Two levels of the Buddhist teaching. "Closed": all phenomena are empty, without fixed identity. "Open": all phenomena are the impressions of the One Reality.

"The pure wind" symbolizes the teaching of enlightenment.

58: Raise your level of insight

Up in the teaching hall, Stone River gave line-by-line comments on a famous verse:

For thirty years I sought a master swordsman
    How grandiose!
How many times the leaves fell and the shoots grew!
    He pretends to be dotty.
But ever since I once saw some peach blossoms
    What about it?
I have never doubted any more
    Too bad he settles down here.

"In this congregation of mine, there are more than seven hundred people: their minds are sputtering with dissatisfaction, their mouths bursting to speak out. Does anyone see what is unfair in this?"
Stone River slapped the meditation bench and said:
"Each of you will have to raise your level of insight enough to see."

59: The Same as Always

Up in the teaching hall Stone River said:
"In the Path of the ancestral teachers, there are carp on the mountain and there is thick dust at the bottom of the well. You must be certain that the kernel of the thousand year peach is the same always as it was of old."
Stone River held up the whisk and said:
"What is it like, everyone?"
Then he left the teacher's seat.

NOTES

"The kernel of the thousand year peach" The gist of the Buddha Dharma.

60: The Bequest of Enlightenment

At a state ceremony, a monk came forward [quoting Zen sayings to ask about their meaning]. The monk said: "'Speak a phrase where the buddhas cannot speak, and every phrase looks to the source. Take a step where the buddhas cannot go, and every step is in touch [with reality].' What is the phrase where the buddhas cannot speak?"

Stone River said, "The literary brilliance is already showing."

The monk continued, "What is the step where the buddhas cannot go?"

Stone River said, "The pure wind circles the earth."

The monk continued, "I remember [this story]. A monk asked Master Fuchang, 'How is it before the golden raven [true *yang*] comes forth?' Fuchang said, 'Everyone looks up in expectation.' What did he mean?"

Stone River said, "A fine meditation saying!"

The monk continued, "When asked, 'How is it after the golden raven comes forth?' Fuchang said, 'Ten thousand lands all observe its light.' What about this?"

Stone River said, "The public case is here right now."

The monk went on, "At just such a time, how should we salute [the Emperor]?"

Stone River said, "We vow to take the pure teaching and serve the Sage Enlightened Lord always."

The monk bowed.

Stone River at that point said, "[Buddha] held up a flower, [Kashyapa] smiled, communicating nothing but the principle of seeing true nature. [Bodhidharma] faced a wall and forgot speech, directly pointed out the essence of pacifying mind. At the moment the bequest is given, how could there be any involvement with calculating thought? When it is taken up face to face, there is no room to hesitate trying to think what to do. Therefore, when one person moves in response, a thousand buddhas share the same source.

"It is like an udambara flower: once it appears, auspicious signs appear in all the realms of the senses and all lands gather in its fragrance. It is like the sun in the east rising into the sky: its pure light shines into every recess and everything in every part of the world has its illumination upon it. It all comes about through a moment of sympathetic penetration [into everything]: naturally the myriad forms of good all gather together.

"How is it at just such a time? We raise our eyes and the azure sky seems washed clean. The golden raven has flown up onto the jade balustrade. Suddenly there's a verse:

> We honor the sage Enlightened Lord of all lands
> With every step he walks on top of Vairocana's head
> One's own Dharmakaya: this is it
> Towering over a thousand ages stirring the fair sound

NOTES

"The golden raven" is the symbol of pure *yang*, which stands for the primordial enlightened awareness of all sentient beings.

"Buddha held up a flower, Kashyapa smiled" This was the beginning of the Zen transmission, in which Buddha wordlessly communicated the gist of his meaning to Kashyapa, who became the first patriarch of Zen in India.

Bodhidharma the twenty-eighth patriarch of Zen in India, who travelled to China to become the first Zen patriarch there.

"The udambara flower" blooms but once in a thousand years: a symbol of the comparative rarity of an enlightened teacher appearing in the world.

Vairocana Buddha, the universal illuminator, representing the one reality pervading everything everywhere.

Dharmakaya, the body of reality, the truth body, of all the buddhas.

"The fair sound" of the Dharma.

61: Then and Now

Profound talk entering into inner truth—the ancients spoke it. Making arrangements for teaching centers—the ancients have functioned like this. The bird's path, the mystic road—the ancients have travelled it. Fancy implements and embroidered bags—the ancients spurned them.

But tell me, what about these days? The fishing pole is totally broken —we're replanting the bamboo. We just get the golden carp's heart, then stop.

NOTES

"The fishing pole" symbolizes the means by which enlightenment is taught.

"The golden carp" symbolizes the enlightened being.

62: Come in out of the rain

Up in the teaching hall Stone River said:

"Buddha Dharma and worldly dharma are pulled over onto one side. The meaning of the Zen patriarchs and the meaning of the scriptural teachings are leaning against a wall. But it has been raining for a long time without clearing: where will patchrobed monks put their leather coats to dry?"

Stone River pointed with his whisk and said:

"Nowhere."

NOTES

"Pulled over onto one side . . . leaning against a wall . . . raining for a long time without clearing" symbols of the decline of the Buddhist institutions.

"Patchrobed monks" Zen monks.

63: True Basis or Misguided Understanding

At midsummer, Stone River went up to the teaching hall and said:

"Everyone, we have set a time period of ninety days to get realization. Now it is already midsummer. The past forty-five days were already gone yesterday. The next forty-five days start today.

"Brothers, within this interval, has there been practice, realization, attainment, and awakening or not? Has [your effort] been a true basis [for enlightenment] or misguided understanding? Come forth with your throat and lips blocked off and say a phrase. Detach from seeing and hearing and feeling and knowing and launch a device. Say a phrase and set heaven and earth turning. Launch a device and make demons and spirits howl.

"I want to know, so we can avoid burying our grievances: is there a lament for passing the whole summer in vain?"

After a long silence Stone River said:

"There is. 'He must not go by night: he must arive in daylight.'"

NOTES

"Midsummer" The Buddhist custom was for monks and nuns to gather together for a summer retreat of intensive meditation work.

"He must not go by night: he must arrive in daylight." The enlightened person must not stay absorbed in the bliss of emptiness ("night"): he must function as a bodhisattva in the world of differentiation ("daylight").

64: Buddha Ocean

A message came that by imperial order Stone River had been granted the sobriquet Fohai 'Buddha Ocean.' After saluting the Emperor, Stone River said:

"The Tao goes beyond ordinary sentiments. Zen transcends number and measure. Since Zen transcends number and measure, how can we study it? Since the Tao goes beyond ordinary sentiments, how can we learn it? Where neither words nor silence reach, where patterns do not yet show, that is where we can comprehend overall.

"It is like the sky, covering everything, like the earth, supporting everything. Like the rain and dew, it makes everything grow. Like the sun and moon, it illuminates everything. All the continents and all the oceans receive its awe-inspiring spiritual radiance. All the plants and all the animals, birds, and fish receive the power of its benevolence.

"I was born in West Shu [Sichuan] and respectfully studied the southern school [Zen]. For eighty years I have drunk when thirsty and eaten when hungry . . .

"How can I speak the phrase that recognizes and repays the benevolence? Heaven is high and the myriad patterns are correct. The ocean is broad and the hundred rivers flow into it."

65: The Solitary Lamp

Stone River cited this case:

"A monk asked Xianglin, 'What is the single lamp inside the room?' Xianglin said, 'If three people testify to it, a land tortoise becomes a sea turtle.'"

Stone River added a verse:

The solitary lamp inside the room you can only know for yourself
To enter the stream [of enlightenment] you must master the move
    that cuts off the streams [of delusion]
One arrowhead which reaches to the sky, outside the triple barrier
The jade rabbit and the golden raven don't dare fly

NOTES

"The jade rabbit and the golden raven" here stand for the moon and the sun.

66: Turn a Somersault

Seeing off old man Yimo on his trip to Zhejiang, Stone River cited a verse by Zen master Zhaozhou, and gave line by line comments:

"'Where there's a buddha, do not stay.' The iron whip shatters the tree of coral.

"'Where there is no buddha, quickly pass by.' A clear pond has no room for the blue dragon to recline.

"'Three thousand miles away, do not misquote it.' He raises his eyebrows, his eyes alert and firm. If so, then he does not go. The misty waters of a hundred cities are hard to depict.

"'Picking willow branches, picking willow branches' This does not allow for [any hesitation]: a blink of the eye and you have forgotten your home.

"Fundamentally a thousand suns are hanging from Zhaozhou's tongue: even sparks struck from stone or flashes of lightning cannot overtake them. To know how to return when the candle is blown out, is still a second level device in our family. Turn a somersault and pull down the birds and the creeping vines: do not consent to stay in the traps of the thousand sages. When has the pillar [the oneness] ever blocked the feeble waves [the multiplicity]? Greatly fanning the true wind, it fills the universe."

67: To the Old Man of the Mountain Stream

When the water level dropped he knew the dipper handle was long
From this the family style grew ever cooler

Sometimes waves arise where there is no wind
Observed coldly, the person who cuts off the stream is keeping
   himself busy

NOTES

"Waves without wind" Metaphor for efforts to communicate the Dharma,
which is fundamentally inexpressible, yet constantly taught by all things at
all times.

"The person who cuts off the stream is keeping himself busy"   After awakening,
and the realization that all phenomena are the marks of the one reality, there
is no further need for the beginners' practice of cutting off contact with sensory
experience, which no longer poses any obstruction to correct perception.

68: Three Dot Ox

The lifeline of patchrobed monks is the eye on the forehead
Open it up and for no reason horns grow on your head
More fortunate still, the fields in the family garden are secure
Where you find a place to till deeply, till deeply

NOTES

"The eye on the forehead" The eye of enlightenment.

"Horns grow on your head" Metaphor for the breakthrough to enlightenment.

"The family garden" The basic endowment of the Zen family, the tradition
of correct practice and true teaching.

69: The Buddhas of the Present

   Seeing off Zen man Hui of Da-zhou going to see Zen master Wuzhun
on Mount Jingshan, Stone River offered this verse:

With horns on his forehead, his eyes grow sinews
Who is the number one body of the buddhas of the present?
Leaving here he burns incense, bows three times and rises
Stop that heretic from inciting the people

NOTES

"His eyes grow sinews" metaphor for developing enlightened perception.

70: Sword Hall

Ordinarily it does not show a phrase with a sharp point
Cold and severe as wind and frost, its majesty is complete
    of itself
Before his foot crosses the threshold he has already observed it
How could he know he's already lost what's in front of his skull?

71: Seeing off Zen man Jinzhou

The great being polishes a brick, his eyes paralyzed
As he goes back, we call in a loud voice to wake him up
What a scene of beating the cart [instead of the horse]!
For no reason it has been wrongly entrusted to the
    horse's colt

NOTES

"Polishing a brick" Seeking enlightenment through meditation alone.

"The horse's colt" A member of the Zen tradition descended from Mazu, Baizhang, and Huangbo.

72: Pure Mountain Stream

Inches away, there's a road through the source of Zen
Why does the swimming fish make himself lose the track?
There is a sound to convey him to the uncommon place
No room at all for any dust or mud

NOTES

"The uncommon place" the realm of enlightenment.

73: Seeing off Xinfeian

If you affirm what is, the golden carp is still stuck in the water
If you deny what is not, the lion turns a flip
The propitious spot on the mountain is outside affirmation and denial
Whom does the Buddha Dharma rely on to be the master?

NOTES

"The golden carp" symbol of the enlightened person.

"The lion" symbol of transcendent wisdom, which takes in both the absolute level and the provisional level of imaginary and relative realities.

74: Moon Pond

The immaculate pure light is shining cold
How many times have you dragged through it creating waves?
Whom will we rely on to tell this to Hanshan?
Don't think our hearts are all alike

NOTES

Hanshan, the famous Buddhist poet of the Tang dynasty.

75: No Image

Blank and empty, before moving the lines
No picking them out singly or joining them together
The era of Great Peace must be like this
When a master of the trigrams meets people, he must not cast
    them at random

NOTES

"Moving the lines . . . the trigrams" of the Book of Changes.

"Great Peace" The classical Chinese term for utopia.

76: What a Perch

Seeing off a monk on his way to East Zhejiang, Stone River gave this verse:

The place where you cannot tread: what a perch!
Soft as iron, hard as mud
You can look everywhere in Jinling, but you won't find it
It's surely west of the east ridge on Traders' Peak

NOTES

Jinling the major metropolis of the area, modern Nanking, an ancient political and cultural center.

Trader's Peak a mountain-island entrepot off the Zhejiang coast, the haunt of smugglers and pirates.

77: The Snow White Ox

He stands out far far away: we cannot overtake him
Time and again he walks through the wild grasses of remote villages
His one-color hide and hair has all changed
His load must be these sentient beings

78: The Iron Wall

Even with heaven and earth for a furnace, we cannot melt through it
Where it does not let the wind through nevertheless, it does let the
    wind through
Only after you have penetrated through it and then come back
Will you see it has one layer after another

79: Words to Open up Everyone Everywhere

Gather up the fallen flowers and stick them back on the branches
    where they were

The wandering bees and the dancing butterflies will fly in thick
    profusion
Don't tell me to smell what has no odor
Full of shame, you are still going back by the old road

80: What's in a Name

To a practitioner changing his name from Deshan to Dezhi, Stone
River wrote:

In our school there is only one Deshan: the whole world looks up
to him with respect. Over the great expanse of several hundred years
his pure wind comes to us without end. Up till now you have had the same
name as him. This was never [intended as] a violation of the taboo on
the names of the dead. [Rather, its true usefulness was this:] Whenever
anyone called to you in front of people, [hearing the name "Deshan"]
unconsciously stirred the ears of the assembly.

The Book of Changes takes [the word] *gen* as 'mountain' *shan.*
The Dictionary takes *gen* as 'stopping' *zhi.* Better take 'stopping' [as
in De-zhi] and change it into 'mountain' [as in De-shan]: just move
one stroke. We must honor our worthy predecessors and be like this.

NOTES

"Only one Deshan" namely Deshan Xuanqian [781-867], teacher of Xuefeng
and Yantou, ancestor of the Yunmen and Fayan houses of Zen.

81: To Qian Yanshou of Tiantong

When there's a good doctor in the house, the diseases are more
    numerous
When there's no place to stop and moor, it's most difficult to
    understand
Water blue as indigo, flowers like silver brocade
As before the sound of [water from] the rafters dripping on the
    old nest

82: Reprinting a Zen classic

For the reprinting of the words of the great Zen teacher Dahui Zonggao [d. 1163] (also called Miaoxi) Stone River wrote this:

What flowed out from Miaoxi's breast:
Letters from the hand of the Doubly Resplendent Son of Heaven
The galaxy will crumble, but this will not
This printing from new blocks is hereby sanctioned

83: Eulogy for a Dead Monk

When the bones of the head monk Yuan of Feng-an were being put into a stupa, Stone River offered this verse:

His spine was hard as iron
It could not be bent for seventy years and more
He fell into the forge at Bell Mountain
And was refined into snowflakes in the torrid sky
I want to take a cloth with no threads
To gather the bones in and wrap them up
I'm afraid they cannot be wrapped
I want to scatter and store them in a seamless stupa
I'm afraid they cannot be stored
Ultimately, how is it?
Feng-an, Feng-an!
You better decide for yourself

84: Where knowledge does not reach

Where knowledge does not reach:
Completely hidden, completely revealed
Going back and forth, getting through from the side
It's still the same as defilement
Using all your strength to leap out

The whole body is within
The one room is vacant and unused all day long
You still have to lock it up and race out on the road

85: Verse at the Cremation of Senior Monk Qing

Immaculate purity
Vast infinity
This source of sickness
Flows on without stopping
Night comes and we utterly overturn it
A torch in front of every family's gate

86: Verse for a Dead Man

When the burial niche was opened for estate manager Jian, Stone River gave this verse:

The solid esoteric body
Depends on *nothing*
In every atom of dust
It abides like this

If estate manager Jian can hold fast to the locked barrier, I guarantee the moon is round at his door.

NOTES

"The solid esoteric body" the Dharmakaya.

"The moon" symbol of the one reality.

87: Be Quick to Awaken

At the cremation of senior monk Jiao, Stone River gave this verse:

Do not worry about thoughts arising,
Just fear you will be slow to awaken

Awakening is itself a disease
What medicine can cure it?
Abandon everything, don't think about it
When refined gold goes into the fire it naturally glitters

NOTES

"Awakening is itself a disease" if the student clings to the experience, making it the antithesis of ordinary life.

"When refined gold goes into the fire it naturally glitters" When enlightened mind enters the mundane realm, it shines with wisdom and compassion.

88: A Spring Tune

At the cremation of attendant Zong, Stone River spoke this verse:

This school of ours
Is hardest to find
But to find it is easy
What's hard is to transmit it
Hard, so hard
West of the city wall
    the white snow spreads a spring tune
Today it gives us one note clearly

He threw down the torch and said, "Quick! Look!"

89: On the Pathways of Mind

At the cremation of duty distributor Hai, Stone River spoke a verse:

On the pathways of mind, green moss grows
At the ocean gate, red flames rise
In your forty-four years,
You have just come here
But here is still not it
The Brahman Excellent Warmth
Is in a mass of fire on the mountain of swords

Looking at you, duty distributor Hai,
As you take the stage to perform your play

NOTES

"Duty distributor" *wei-na* was one of the officers in the community of monks.

"The mountain of swords" a place of punishment in hell.

90: Buddha Subduing Demons

(Stone River wrote this to go with a painting of Buddha subduing demons)

When Buddha first appeared in the world, demons and outsiders were flourishing. There was a demon-mother with a thousand children of many different kinds who fed on people's sons and daughters. Devas and humans were afflicted by this. So Buddha took her favorite child and covered it with a crystal bowl. When the demon-mother discovered her child was lost, she wept and wailed and searched everywhere. Buddha called her to approach him, and pointed to her child for her to take back. The demon-mother mobilized all the demon-soldiers at her command, but with all their supernatural powers, they could not move the bowl. Buddha asked her, "Is your beloved child the same as the beloved children of other people, or is it different?"

The demon-mother repented, gave thanks, and bowed in homage. She vowed that from that time onward, whenever she saw other people's sons and daughters, she would regard them as her own; and if people were seeking sons and daughters, she would help them in their prayers. As soon as she made the vow, the bowl [covering her child] lifted up by itself, and she took her child in her arms and departed.

If the Dharma is ten feet high, delusion is ten feet high. It's just that crooked and straight are divergent paths. The tradition says [of sentient beings]: As soon as the slightest thought is born, they are controlled by sensory experience. They are placed among palaces of delusion and dens of demons. They go through the long dark night dreaming with eyes closed. [Delusion] reaches everywhere.

Buddha felt compassion for them, so he used the light of great wisdom, like the sun hanging in the sky, and destroyed the darkness, letting all sentient beings open their eyes and see clearly, so they abandon the crooked and return to the straight.

The painter from his brush-tip samadhi has produced as if by magical illusion this picture of Buddha subduing the demons. There is deep intent in this. If in this picture you can suddenly see before the thoughts of good and evil and wrong and right are formed, then who is Buddha? Who is [the great deluder] Mara? If you still cannot see, then better alert yourself.

(dated: 1245, Tiger Hill)

91: The True Lifeline

In 1255 at Mount Jingshan Stone River wrote this verse as part of a preface to an edition of the canon by Tan Shao-yun of Yu-zhou, revised by Zen man Ming of Siming:

In the true lifeline personally transmitted by the buddhas
    and enlightened teachers
The scribe of Yu-zhou has discovered the deepest source
Glittering rays of light ten times ten thousand fathoms high
All that's important is for a connoisseur to transmit the
    single seal

92: A Thousand Times is not Too Much

Stone River addressed this verse to Zen man Chun of Jiujiang who was going back to Donglin Temple to receive ordination:

For years the Buddha Dharma has brought with it parts that
    are hard to understand
Trying to figure them out a thousand times is not too much
I send word to Donglin slightly raising my hand
I see how your eye and brain are

Comment by Deming of Ashoka Temple:
"Old man Stone River of Lingyin in his verse to see of Zen man Chun went beyond the scope of people's ideas. The light of his writing

illuminates present and past. The parts that are hard to understand
in the Buddha Dharma: do those with eyes and brains discern them?"

Comment in verse by Deru of Mount Lu:
>   Stone River tried to figure them out a thousand times
>   Later generations tried to figure them out a thousand times
>   This is not what's hard to understand in the Buddha Dharma
>   This is just trying to figure it out a thousand times.

Comment in verse by Yunyou of Tiantong Temple:
>   The long broad tongue of the mountain stream
>   Flows on constantly day and night
>   This is not perception in the eye
>   Who recognizes this chapter and verse?

93: Knowing Satisfaction

>   I have a square field
>   Within it the myriad entanglements all cease
>   Though the living shore is tranquil
>   Daily activities are not in vain
>   Knowing satisfaction, long years of joy
>   Without seeking, everywhere is Zen
>   Neighbors to the west know this meaning
>   Pines and bamboo melt from view in the cold mist

94: Returning through the Clouds

>   Pulling along clouds, following the dragon, going and returning
>   Mindless, but it seems like mind is there
>   Just because I fear losing my restraint
>   I never throw open my cliffside room

95: The Smell of Sweat

>   We are never aware of the smell of our own sweat
>   But before we open our mouths, the others already know

The smell reaches the two stone buddhas of Su-zhou:
One covers his nose, one knits his brow

96: Standing Out

Standing out a ten thousand feet above the ordinary
Rising like a wall, solitary and steep, impossible to climb
South, north, east, west, gazing up in vain
Who knows that each and every step we take is within it

97: One Root

Heaven & earth have the same root: they go back to a
    single finger
For you three or four is already too many
Carefree and at ease, raising a fist
How can counting count that?

98: Who are they? Who are we?

Born in the Tathagata's family
One must study the Tathagata's practice
All thoughts enter correct mindfulness
All contention is returned to non-contention
The buddha-land at Shaolin will not appear again
The great assembly on Taishan can be relied on
Who are they? Who are we?
You need a flash of sudden insight

NOTES

Tathagata epithet of the Buddha.

Shaolin where Bodhidharma communicated the Zen message to his Chinese
successor Huike early in the sixth century.

Taishan one of the sacred mountains of Chinese Buddhism.

99: To a Monk Returning Home to Visit Sick Parents

Ten forms of non-returning, but today you are returning
You did not wish to see them again, but today you are seeing
    them again
Ancient and modern, the Great Path is always calm and even
Each one of us must put through a line to its gate

100: Which is Which?

In an atom of dust, a galaxy of worlds
In a half a second, eighty thousand springs
Going and coming like this, staying like this
No one knows which is the host, which is the guest

NOTES

"The host" represents the fundamental, the primary, the absolute truth level.

"The guest" represents the derivative, the secondary, the relative reality level.

101: Coping with Reality

When seeing off the monk Hui, Stone River spoke this verse:

Shaving off his black hair and putting on a monk's robe
Scriptures and prayer beads always by his side
He wants to reach the mysterious gate and study the true self
He should look at Shiji's visit to Judi

NOTES

"Shiji's visit to Judi" (This story is in case 19 of the Blue Cliff Record.) When
Judi was first living in a hermitage, a nun named Shiji ("Reality") came to his
hut. She went straight in, and without taking off her hat, she walked three
times around the seat where Judi was meditating and said, "If you can speak,
I'll take off my rain hat." She repeated this three times, but Judi had no reply.
As she was leaving, Judi invited her to stay. The nun said, "If you can speak,
I'll stay over." Again Judi had no reply. The nun walked out. Judi sighed and
said, "Though I inhabit the body of a man, I lack a man's spirit." After this he
aroused his will to clarify the great matter of enlightenment.

102: To a Lost Wanderer

Do not wander in the marketplace of verbal hairsplitting
Do not follow people trying a thousand times to divine the answer
Another day, if we have an affinity, we will meet again
The golden-haired lion must be groaning

NOTES

"The golden-haired lion" Manjushri, the bodhisattva of transcendent wisdom, rides upon a golden-haired lion, which represents the interpenetration of absolute and relative realities.

103: It's Facing You

Seeing off the Taoist master Li, Stone River gave this verse:

Carefully investigating the five thousand words of the *Dao De Jing*
Each and every word is taught in your house
If you want to know the most abstruse meaning
It's facing you, neutral and pure: there is nothing else at all

104: One Flavor Zen

One flavor Zen—peppery and pungent
Getting used to it is not a matter for the spoon,
    [but for the palate]
The teacher of fifteen hundred students:
His words are already perfect
    before he comes out the gate

105: Bequeathed to Whom?

Putting it on is the same as taking it off
Observe well Shiji's visit to Judi
For over five hundred years up till now
A single expanse of wind and light—bequeathed to whom?

NOTES

"Shiji's visit to Judi" see the note to #101.

106: Our Old Home

Situated in the realm of sensory troubles, abiding in deep Zen
How many times has the heart of compassion been shattered, then
      made whole again?
Gain and loss, affirmation and denial all abandoned
Everywhere it's all the scenery of our old home

107: The Whole Face is Revealed

At a memorial service, when he was about to hang the portrait of
the deceased Master Shitian, Stone River spoke this verse:

A whisp of cloud on south mountain
A drop of water from west lake
The whole face is revealed
Where can you avoid it?
If you think it is old man Shitian
A thousand miles away you are face to face
If you think it is not old man Shitian
Face to face you are a thousand miles away
Is it or is it not?

Then Stone River unrolled the portrait and said: "It's all right here.
Stop arguing about bubbles being born and bubbles disappearing. Cherish
the pure wind that circles the earth."

108: Lamentation for Master Wuzhun

"Coming empty and alone, he blocked off empty space so it could
not be pushed off. Going bare and naked, he piled up mountain ranges
with nowhere to put them. But being this way is still the very first device,
it's not the last word. But what is the very last word?"
Stone River looked around at the audience [and exclaimed]:
"Heavens! Heavens! Wrongful suffering!"

NOTES

"The first device" The methods provisionally employed to introduce people to the Buddha Dharma; typically the teaching that all things are impermanent, and that detachment is the route out of suffering.

"The last word" The full expression of the Buddha Dharma, the reality that is beyond all concepts, encompassing without dualism the absolute unity and the relative multiplicity.

"Wrongful suffering" The suffering of sentient beings is illusory, and unnecessary: the product of their own conditioned perceptions and attachments.

109: Offering Tea for Elder Zhengjiao of Iron Stupa

Sleeping eyes in the middle of the night are really
    lost and numb
Returning in a dream, o so far, but still not getting home
Having searched through the writings of masters everywhere
    and plumbed their secrets
It's just worth a bowl of bitter astringent tea

Here [in death] Elder Zhengjiao witnesses the lifeline [of enlighten-ment]. In years past we met in True Awakening Hall without meeting. Today we part at the Nirvana Platform without parting. Though it is so, I carefully pour out this bowl of tea, body turning quickly in the mass of searing flames.

NOTES

"Tea" in Zen lore, tea is associated with wakefulness.

110: Remembering the Enlightened Ancestors

Stone River gave this talk at a small gathering in honor of the deceased Master Wuji.

"In our school there are no words, nor is there any dharma to give to people. That's why Deshan hit and Linji shouted as soon as people entered the gate. It's like beating the poison-drum, like holding the [deadly sword] 'Diamond King'. Those who hear the drum perish, those who hesitate before the sword are lost.

"But if we went on this way all the time, the Path would be cut off and bereft of people. Although officially there's no room to let a needle through, unavoidably we open up another road. It may be two thousand years ago or ten thousand miles away, but we meet in person face to face.

"Hahaha! Someone comes from Jiangxi to report that the Cloud Mass Peak at Yangshan is standing shoulder to shoulder with Lotus Society Peak at Lushan: they are going off together to central India, to Kushinagara, where right now it's the fifteenth day of the second month, and old Yellow Face [Buddha] is about to enter final nirvana: lying in his golden coffin he speaks a verse: 'All compounded things are impermanent, the phenomena of birth and extinction. When birth and extinction are extinct, nirvana is bliss.' When he died his golden body was burned in the samadhi fire: in this fire appeared indestructible diamond relics, not [perishable bone fragments] like ours.

"Let's go back and visit Great master Bodhidharma on Bear Ear Mountain. We lower our heads and ask if he is well. We raise our eyes to take a look, but the Master is already in the Congling Range [on his way back to India], one shoe in hand, carefree and content, going off alone. So we go up to him and ask, 'Why are you acting so careless? Will you favor us with a word?' He says, 'Five mouths go together, nine tens without "them" and "us".' Then he points with his finger and says, 'What can they do about Great Master Caoqi [Huineng, the sixth patriarch of Zen]? He is returning to [his native backwoods] Xin-zhou in disguise. Better go accompany him.'

"The great teacher [Caoqi] hears his words, lifts his hand and waves and says, 'When leaves fall they come back to the root of the tree. In times to come there will be no mouth [to preach the Dharma].' This made old man Wuji of South Mountain unable to hold back his mirth: he found a brush and wrote a verse that said:

Sixty-four years
Angry at the buddhas and patriarchs
Wholly transformed with one laugh
Emptiness alone revealed

"So then [Wuji] rode [his teacher] Huiri's tower upside down out the triple gate, crossed over West Lake and sadly departed forever."

Stone River gave a shout and said: "Cloud Mass Peak returns to Yangshan, Lotus Society Peak returns to Lushan." He held up the staff and said: "Though my staff does not enter their shrine, in the path of humanity and righteousness I still must assist in the mourning [for them]." Then he brandished the staff.

Stone River also cited this case:

"A monk asked Nanyuan: 'Where have all the sages since antiquity gone to?' Nanyuan said, 'If not to heaven, then to hell.' The monk said, 'What about you, Master?' Nanyuan said, 'Do you know where I am?' The monk hesitated trying to think of something to say. Nanyuan hit him across the mouth with the whisk, then summoned him closer and said, 'The imperative is for you to practice,' then hit him again.

"Xuedou commented: 'The imperative operates on its own, but the whisk does not know where it's coming from. I would call it blind, but this is adding frost to snow.'"

Stone River said: "If it's right, it's the function of the whole potential. If it's wrong, it's taking advantage of power to cheat people. If you know where Wuji is, you know where all the sages since antiquity are at. Where are they right now?"

After a silence, Stone River said: "They do not remain in the station of buddhas and patriarchs: they go among devas and humans without any preconceived arrangements."

111: Do you want to see?

At the ceremony when the bones of the Master of Zhantang were put into the stupa, Stone River said:

"Right where we are, eternal profound clarity. If you look for it, it cannot be seen. Do you want to see?"

Stone River held up the bones and said, "These are what was picked up of the Master of Zhantang out of the flying sparks and flames [of the funeral pyre]. They have fallen into my hands. Ultimately, how will I pass them on? Where sun and moon do not reach, the Master of Zhantang wants you to be quick about it and transform your being."

112: Under a Shadowless Tree

Stone River spoke this verse at the cremation of estate overseer Tan:

In years gone by he was lord of the estate
He knew all about the fields and gardens of his ancestors
At midnight neither men nor oxen appear
This is just when the moon is bright
Don't pursue the Final Phrase
Seventy-five years [under] a shadowless tree:
Look at him inside the fire pulling off branches

NOTES

"At midnight" is a metaphor for meditation on emptiness.

"When the moon is bright" when enlightenment becomes manifest.

"The Final Phrase" the totality, reality-as-is, encompassing both absolute and relative.

113: When the Lotus Opens

Stone River spoke this verse at the cremation of Hermit Qian:

Worldly affairs blazing like a mass of fire
Old Qian knew all about each and every one
But now he has switched his step and changed his body
This is precisely the time when the lotus opens and buddha appears

114: Flying Sparks

Stone River spoke this verse at the cremation of storehouse supervisor Gu:

Deep and strong and mysterious and far:
Those who arrive know its extent.
As for storehouse supervisor Gu,
His whole body is in this.

Among bluegreen mountains and white clouds,
Amidst purple smoke and red flames,
The scattering flying sparks are all in you.

115: Close Continuity

Stone River spoke this verse at the cremation of temple super-intendent Gen:

Sixty-four years of close continuity
Following the square and round
Getting lost halfway there
Clouds roll up and rain scatters
The iron boat reaches the shore
The moon descends across the blue sky
Its face as before
Spring wind over the river country in April and May
The flowering plants and blossoming trees are vying in beauty

Stone River called out, "Superintendent Gen!" He drew a circle in the air and said, "How is it when this one suddenly functions?" Then he threw down the torch and said, "Just look!"

116: Light as a Feather

At the cremation of the architect Zhen, Stone River gave this verse:

Zen man Zhen of Jian-guan
Accomplished great work
His actions were light as a feather
But his achievements were heavy as a mountain
For thirty years he was like this
He helped Fojian build a new monastery
He was with Fojian but did not share in [his wisdom]
For this Great Enlightenment Hall of ours
The work was planned by him
How could he expect that his time would arrive
And suddenly he would depart forever?

Architect Zhen!
The eternal rain is about to clear, but has not cleared yet
At your place we regretfully seek a spark of fire

NOTES

"The eternal rain" The habit-energy of the age-old ignorance that keeps sentient beings deluded.

117: Spirit Traces

Stone River offered this eulogy as the bones of the mountain-master Sheng were being put in his stupa:

"With lofty virtue over the years, his perception was illuminated and perfected. In his youth he studied in earnest and served teachers to the limit of his powers. In his later years he dwelled on a mountain [as a recluse] and in response to the potentials [of students] adapted accordingly. He conjured up the spirit traces of a majestic golden buddha and magically produced jade towers and palaces. One day his merit was complete and the fruits [of his practice] full. With the sound of stones knocking together, he passed on the teaching and returned [to the source]. A stalk of grass was left after his cremation.

"But I must give a verdict." He held up the bones and said, "Mountain-master Sheng: he could not be pressed together, he could not be pulled apart. Let's let him make a mess on his empty hillside."

NOTES

"Make a mess" This is how the Zen school spoke of meditational work resulting in magical apparitions. According to Zen teachings, ecstatic visionary experiences may be the by-product of meditation, but are not its aim.

118: Essays in the Void

Stone River gave this verse at the cremation of Secretary Kang:

From west to east, from east to west
Every step is entirely right
Every step is still wrong

Fully awake, you remember the time when you arrived home
Your three hundred previous essays
Were all done in vain when you got here
Let them go in the void,
Think no more about them
The stone man on the mountain ridge is singing a song
The metal buddha who has passed through fire raises his eyebrows

119: A True Son

Stone River gave this verse at the cremation of water keeper Fazhen:

A true son of the [teacher's private] room on Shuang-Jing Mountain
How could he have been the same as people wandering outside the gate?
With every step he took, he was home
With everythought, correct concentration
Sometimes he abandoned the pure and entered the polluted
Sometimes he cast off the polluted and upheld the pure
He was on both sides, but he did not stay on either side
His wordplay was never wordplay
Water Keeper Fazhen!
The Fire-God is inviting you:
He wants you to talk about your Zen diseases

120: Right Now You Look Very Fiery

Stone River gave this verse at the cremation of Mr. Yu, general manager of the temple lands:

General manager Yu!
East of the stream, west of the stream
Head of the fields, tail of the fields
Letting to, gathering in
No land at all empty or abandoned
Upholding practice like this
Serving as a model like this
The principle and the interest appear ready-made

Stop coveting more land
General manager Yu:
When we look on coldly, right now you look very fiery

121: Look for No-Place

    Stone River gave this verse at the cremation of stupa-master An:

Stupa-master! Stupa-master!
I too will put down a turning word.
How did he live?
A golden-haired lion in his den
A fierce tiger concealed in the forest
His awe-inspiring wind was solemn and severe
His claws and teeth never showed
He was like this for eighty years
There's no place at all to look for him
Look for no-place—that's where he lives
Stupa-master An!
Right now, in the roaring flames of the pyre
Boldly apply your energy and spirit:
You better find out for yourself!

122: In Flames of Fire

    At the cremation of the master of the canon Zhen Shiqi gave this verse:

Teacher and pupil meet
Three calls, three responses
[Stone River held up the
torch]
Relying on this one
The whole great treasury of scriptural teachings
Is set forth and taken in
[he again held up the torch]
Relying on this one too
All the buddhas of past present and future

In flames of fire
Turn the great wheel of the Dharma
What do you rely on, master of the canon Zhen?
Boldly apply your energy and spirit:
Do not let yourself stumble past [and miss your chance]

123: Subtle Touch

Stone River gave this verse at the cremation of bathkeeper Chao:

[When the bodhisattvas went in to bathe]
They did not wash off the dust
They did not wash off their bodies
Subtle touch communicated illumination
And they attained the station of children of Buddha
They just knew the peace within this station:
They still did not understand that there is no cool spot in a
    boiling cauldron
Bathkeeper Chao! Do you understand?
Better comprehend in the flames of the fire

NOTES

"When the bodhisattvas went in to bathe" A story from the Surangama Sutra,
the basis of case #78 of the Blue Cliff Record. The bodhisattvas filed in to bathe
and all were suddenly enlightened.

124: Grandpa's Gate

Stone River gave this verse at the cremation of temple super-
intendent Shao:

Do you want to know old grandpa's gate?
Inheriting it is easy, but living up to it is hard
Living up to it is easy, but protecting it is hard
Hard, hard:
The walls of the room all block the way
Easy, easy:

The pure wind sweeps the earth
Superintendent Shao! Do you know yet or not?
In front of the gate of every house, the torch

NOTES

"The walls of the room" the limitations of conditioned consciousness.

"The pure wind" the omnipresent enlightening influence of reality.

125: A True Seedling

At the cremation of the keeper of the shrine Yi, Stone River said:
"There is no buddha in the ancient shrine: every day fragrant smoke,
every night a lamp. The holy sound from India, how did it come? It
took a true seedling of Shaolin [to receive it]. One could say that if
you do righteous deeds, this is the awakened mind. What does this
mean? If you do unrighteous deeds, this is the mind of confusion. What
does this mean?

"Keeper of the shrine Yi was not constrained by being or by
nothingness: mind and body washed clean, just spontaneously so. Now
he comes back among the flames and shows a lotus flower."

NOTES

"A true seedling of Shaolin" A true successor of Bodhidharma, the first
patriarch of Zen in China, who taught at Shaolin.

126: Flying Above the Peaks

At the ceremony of spreading earth over the bones of the lecturer
Tong-an, Stone River said:

"Amidst the sameness of the myriad phenomena, there is difference.
The undifferentiated whole is within a single hermitage. But now sameness and difference are both taken away, and he strides along cutting
them off as if flying above the highest peaks.

"I humbly hope that the great lecturer and general supervisor of monks Tong-an, who has newly entered perfect peace, will come riding on his vows of compassion, and thus come without coming, and that he will abide on the basis of these vows of compassion, and thus abide without abiding.

"From a nonabiding basis, he showed achievements in the realm of compounded things. He used discipline, concentration and wisdom to make his own existence impeccable, and pointed out the [meditation perspectives] of emptiness, provisional existence, and the mean, to benefit younger students. He relied on the gate of the scriptural teachings, and relocated several times to preside [over teaching assemblies].

"Though [sometimes] we say there is a Path that can be transmitted, this is like a glittering carp being stuck in the water. Really there is no Dharma that can be expounded: it's like a multicolored phoenix soaring through the clouds.

"Sixty-nine years [Tong-an lived]: it was like the time it takes to snap one's fingers. Talking and smiling, satisfied and content, he rolled up his robe and went. Beyond the clouds, his heavenly fragrance is poignant, solitary, still. Among the congregation [his mystical attainments were such that celestial] flowers rain down suddenly making a mess. Everyone thinks that when you reach the river the land of Wu ends: how could they know that on the other side of the shoreline are the many mountains of Yue?

"If you see Tong-an in this, it still won't do. Do you want to see old man Tong-an? If you look inside the reliquary, you will not find him, but you will meet him in the reflections of the white clouds."

NOTES

"A glittering carp stuck in the water" If there is a dualistic sense of attainment, of a separate perceiving subject experiencing a transcendent object, this is still not the perception of the buddhas.

"The land of Wu . . . the mountains of Yue" Everyone thinks that a life of sanctity, deep learning, and meditative accomplishment is the ultimate in holiness, but the path of the enlightening works of the buddhas is endless. (Wu and Yue are neighboring regions on the south China coast.)

127: The Golden Lock Breaks Open

When the reliquary containing the bones of the Korean lecturer Bu-an was opened, Stone River spoke this verse:

A lock with no whiskers locks up the deep blue sky
The lock breaks and you charge out, but the road does not go through
Take care, you non-doing, unconcerned traveller
Don't you know the whole body is within it?
Therefore it is our true lord, the basis of wisdom,
The correct transmission of the Chief of the Good
In a teaching hall in Korea, Lecturer Bu-an:
Seventy-three years fundamentally without coming or going
Hundreds and thousands of samadhis always appearing before him
Whether advancing or retreating, always on the Middle Path
In the realm of a great man, speech and silence, movement and
        stillness
Are all the Dharma-gate of the wondrous principle of true emptiness
Everywhere the Elephant King circles
Everywhere the Lion charges
It is so, it is so:
Stop discussing the moon over the dais
It is not so, it is not so:
Let the polar mountain tumble to the ground
At just such a time, tell me:
Lecturer Bu-an was always within it
Why wasn't he stuck on the one phrase within it?
The golden lock and the mystic barrier break open
A galaxy of scriptures comes forth from an atom of dust

NOTES

"The Middle Path" between the unity of absolute reality and the multiplicity of relative existence.

"The Elephant King, the Lion" symbols of enlightenment.

"The moon over the dais" symbol of the oneness of the absolute.

"Let the polar mountain tumble" do not cling to oneness; do not become attached to the absolute and reject the relative.

"The golden lock and the mystic barrier" Having reached the perception of the oneness of reality, the Zen practitioner must learn to reintegrate the multiplicity of relative phenomena.

128: The Spring Wind Blows Him Away

At the ceremony when the bones of head monk Deng of Qingjing were scattered, Stone River gave this verse:

Even on the summit of the mountain, head monk Deng kept looking
        back to the village garden
Now that his powers of vision are exhausted he's still the same
        anyway
The spring wind over the river country suddenly blows him away
I wonder who this news comes to

Stone River held up a bone and said:
"This is one of the spirit bones of head monk Deng, who was smelted and refined a thousand times in the forge at Qingling. It is hard as metal or stone, and glitters like ice and frost. Let it go, and it engulfs all of space. Gather it in, and everything is here within it. His whole life he was moral and righteous: at the end the climbing vine [of his ceaseless seeking] has fallen into my hands. But tell me, how shall I set it to rest? Inside a limited realm, sun and moon do not reach: outside the conventional square, heaven and earth cycle on by themselves."

129: Penetrate Through This Barrier

At the cremation of workman Chen Daobao (whose name means 'Jewel of the Path'), Stone River gave this verse:

The perfect jewel of the Path:
Where should we search for it?
If we seek inside or out, it has no traces
If we use it in daily activities, this is just right
For thirty-three years

He was the son of the Chen family
But he did not continue the traditional family business
Four, five, six years here at Tian-ning since he left home
But he did not cut down the weeds in front of the shrine
He was not bound by birth and death or going and coming
He did not care about enlightenment or affliction
Even so, he still had to realize that there is the Last Word

Stone River held up the torch and said: "Penetrate through this barrier, and I'll give you the bequest with my own hand."

130: Let the Sparks Fly

At the cremation of the cook Zhijiao, Stone River gave this verse:

If you accomplish the business of leaving home
You are a true home leaver
Washing the rice to remove the sand is not it
Washing the sand to remove the rice is also wrong

Stone River held up the torch and said, "For him we light this fire: let the sparks fly all over the world."

131: Austerities

At the cremation of the workman-ascetic Jingdao, Stone River said:

In leaving home and practicing austerities what's valuable is
    refined cultivation
To dress and eat appropriately and not seek externally
With a stone hung from your waist you grew fond of walking the
    treadmill
You did not notice the bright moon pass by your retreat
Since you have been a guest in our hall at Lingyin
You should take Mr. Lu as a model
If you have not yet illuminated mind and seen your real identity

You will not avoid the boiling pressure of the sufferings of birth
    and death
This year you followed me to Tiger Hill
When sickness enmeshed you, you stopped like this
When you stopped, you stopped completely
Ultimately, where did you go?
So take my torch:
Light comes and light goes: we let you roam free

NOTES

"Take Mr. Lu as a model" Mr. Lu was Huineng, the sixth patriarch of Zen, who was also a workman at a Zen center; Huineng realized complete enlightenment, beyond any dualistic sense of purity and defilement.

"You grew fond of walking the treadmill . . . but did not notice the bright moon pass by your retreat" Stone River criticizes Jingdao for making his asceticism an end in itself, without awakening to the total reality.

132: How to Plant the Bodhi Tree

Stone River gave this verse at the cremation of gardener Lai:

A guest here at Lingyin Hall
Chi-jing Lai served in the garden
Moving his hoe lightly up and down
Getting to the bottom of things without any
    doubts or suspicions
He knew how to take the bodhi tree
And plant it everywhere in the fire
Gardener Lai!
In the furnace the ashes have burned down:
    do not add more fuel
The iron tree without flowers will indeed bloom

NOTES

"The iron tree will indeed bloom" From the emptiness of all phenomena will issue forth the inherent wisdom and compassion of the buddhas.

133: Eulogy for a Princess

In the midst of the formless body, there is a body with form. In the palace of yellow gold, how many times renewed! Turn back and look a hundred years later, and it's all like a dream. Who was the person constructing dreams while awake?

The deceased was the Princess Yu. In forty-nine years she came forth born from the formless, and from the world of form entered extinction. In the intervening time, every time she moved or was still, every time she spoke or was silent, all her goings and comings took place up in the golden palace in front of the jade tower.

But wealth and rank and honor and glory are all ways to serve Buddha [if used properly]. You must realize that within the dream there is one who is not dreaming.

In the old days someone asked, "The physical body decomposes: what is the hard and fast body of reality?" The Zen master replied: "The mountain flowers open like brocade, the waters of the valley stream are blue as indigo."

If you can comprehend here in this, nothing can stop you from walking hand in hand with the worthy women in the sutras. If you hesitate, then listen to a verse:

In the vastness of the dusts, seven precious clusters
    [of consciousness]
But within them is not the place to put the body at peace
In the shadow of the green mountain the white clouds fly
Moving your body with a slow step, again and again you return

Before the world was formed, this field was already there. The womb was ready, and with it Princess Yu. Now the earth and sky are open: wind and light flood the eye. Mountains and rivers on every side: the sense of spring fills the scene. On the morning you enter the tomb, there are sharp pangs of regret at your departure. Your retainers express their farewells. Your dear son bows and turns away. Your kinfolk are smitten with sorrow. But they cannot hold you back or keep you.

At just such a time, it is evident that the princess has buried her jade-like body here without knowing that the children of Buddha inhabit this field. If this is the functioning of a buddha, then who are the children of Buddha? And what are we calling 'this field'? If you receive the use of it here, then you are always within it, whether walking, standing, sitting, or lying down. Buddha-lands and heavens are not outside of Mind: what about the Last Word? All the lands in an atom of dust protect you: your wealth and rank and honor are bequeathed to posterity.

NOTES

"Seven precious clusters" The consciousnesses associated with sight, hearing, taste, smell, touch, the conceptual faculty, and the faculty of synthesis-evaluation-motivation.

"The Last Word" see note to #108.

134: Eulogy for a Buddhist in Government

A single leaf rides the tide and floats over shallows and depths
Asking the way to Shanghai, visiting Sanlin
In the shadows of the river clouds welcoming the land
Ten thousand miles of cultivated fields—one stretch of Mind
So our Mr. Cai, the government officer,
Came from This in the old days
Lived in This his whole life
Made a living and established a career in This
Respectfully served [the Emperor] and solicitously nurtured
    [the common people] in This
Breaking down the fences
Spreading humanity and benevolence
Scrupulously cultivating the perfection of giving
Travelling to all the Zen mountains
All without leaving This
Because of this
His fields and gardens are so broad a duck cannot fly across them
His children and grandchildren are so thick his kinsmen fill
    all before him
And these are not apart from This either
How wonderful! How rare!
His mission has just ended
It was his eighty-first spring
It has been 260 days since he dusted off his clothes and
    returned to the West

After all, the sound of the tide carries sadness
And the echo of the wind holds sorrow
As you are about to face the funeral pyre
We wash your face and waft fragrant incense over you
This is just the time when the lotus opens
Birth and death without regrets
But what about the one move that transforms the body?
At Double Juniper Hermitage we had a pact
To wait and see the udambara flower appear in the flames

Stone River then held up the torch and said, "Do you see? The buddhas of past present and future are right here attaining true enlightenment, sitting in the bodhimandala, emitting a great light that vanquishes all forms of darkness. Right here all the generations of Zen masters are transmitting the school of the Buddha-mind and opening up great forges to melt down and refine ordinary and sage. All the teachers who have found the Path are right here distinguishing truth from error, burning the books of outsiders, and making the correct teaching reach everywhere.

"As for the great patron of Buddhism, Lord Cai Xuanyi: 'When there is a rule, we adhere to the rule. When there is no rule, we follow precedent.' Mr. Cai had a measure of insight. Here today he abandons the segmented body of birth and death, and attains the indestructible esoteric body.

"Under the twin trees [where Buddha died] the golden coffin spontaneously burned. Today at Double Juniper Hermitage, the fragrant fuel has exhausted itself.

"Nevertheless, as for the Last Word: I had a long association with our patron Lord Cai, but today I will say it all anyway."

Stone River held up the torch and said, "Officer Cai, wake up! Mobilize your energy and spirit and comprehend right here."

NOTES

"This" the reality of the enlightened ones.

"Humanity and benevolence" the cardinal virtue of Confucianism, *ren*, human fellow-feeling.

"The bodhimandala" the site of enlightenment.

135: Field of the Immortals

At the burial of Liu Duqin, Stone River said:

A stretch of the immortals' unused field
Who comes today to be its master?
Limitless wind and light have occupied it all
How can it bear the four-season spring of the flowering trees?

Everybody, this cave in the earth already belonged to Mr. Liu even before the primeval chaos was divided. After the primeval chaos was divided, heaven and earth hid it, living spirits guarded it, waiting for this time today, when it is given to Commandant Liu along with the land all around it, to be his eternal resting place. Buddha-lands and heavenly palaces are all here in this: this is the abode of the sons of Buddha. Even the functioning of the buddhas is all within it.

Whether walking, standing, sitting, lying down, make your spirit supple in this. But tell me, where is the true nature of the one spirit? If you comprehend, its face is right here now. If not, then with good rivers and good mountains on all sides, the dense thickets of pine and bamboo draw the pure wind.

NOTES

"The immortals" in Taoist lore, the *xian*, the transformed humans who live forever as repositories of truth.

"Make your spirit supple" Taoist cultivation aims to make the spirit perfectly adaptable and fluid.

136: Zen uses of Literature

In the Zen community we use verses and poems for the extra flavor of the joy of Zen. Huangmei once said: "In this verse, you have not yet seen your true nature." Fayan once said: "With this verse you are worthy to succeed to our school." These are cases of knowing people by their words. Frequently in leisure moments during Zen assemblies, people use a song or a poem to cleanse away karmic consciousness and open the channel to the source of inherent nature. But they never dare to imitate the message of unique illumination. Otherwise they would be wrongly recopying words and phrases: it is obvious that this would do damage to the nurturing of the root of the Path. Everyone studying Zen should be aware of this.

Recently I was on Mount Siming with Elder Fan of Qing-liang and we travelled to Damei Temple, where we came across ten pieces by Momei, the Master 'Light of the Flower of Harmony'.

The verses are entitled:
'Hanging from a cliff, letting go'
'Coming back to life after extinction'
'Spring returns on level ground'
'There is flavor in the flavorless'
'One branch of plum comes out'
'Five leaves join their fragrance'
'High or low as appropriate'
'Free to be straight or crooked'
'The flowers of illusion totally disappear'
'Reality always perfect'

From start to finish the writer uses things to reveal inner truth and explains the process in stages in order to describe the flowing meditation work of the Zen family. He proceeds from entering the Path and responding to the world, to getting the message and returning to the root.

At Shixiang Temple and Changyuan Mountain Zen master Wuzhun commented: "The yellow are yellow by themselves, the green are green by themselves. On each and every branch natural reality appears. Today's sour taste is all forgotten. How can we explain the kernel to other people?"

Embarrassed by my deficiencies, unused to declaiming in verse, I nevertheless force myself to think to where thought cannot reach. After all, have the illusory flowers all disappeared? Does Momei have no place to open his mouth? In the midst of our embarrassment, we unconsciously smile. Ah! Is this 'coming back to life after extinction'? Is it 'spring returns on level ground'? The writer has approached the unapproachable, and come up with 280 words [ten verses, each with four 7-word lines]: he did not pick out the repetitions in the rhymes and meanings of the lines, but just contented himself with not losing the original idea. Dropped into the bag of unconcern, ten views of yellow and green.

One night I was talking by the stove with Gen Yan about this, and he gladly wrote off ten pieces to match [Momei's ten verses], put down his brush, and smiled. Is this cleansing away karmic consciousness? Or is it wrongly copying words and phrases? There must be someone who will cut them away for me.

NOTES

"Karmic consciousness" the ordinary consciousness of sentient beings, conditioned by their actions and the actions of those around them.

"Yellow and green" symbolize the (religiously) ripe and unripe, the realms of the enlightened and the deluded.

137: Who Does not have a Heart?

Stone River wrote this afterword to a copy of the Heart Sutra made by State Minister You Dazi, whose Buddhist name was Layman Guitang:

Ancient and modern, kings and nobles and important men have sometimes inclined toward the Buddhist Path and praised it, and sometimes slandered and vilified it. Though praise an vilification are not the same, it is one and the same Mind. The Surangama Sutra says: "Going along, going against, it's all expedient means."
Here we have 276 words written by Guitang. It is called the Heart Sutra: who does not have a heart? Those who awaken early and those who awaken late all enter this gate. This is how we preach and this is how we write. Decisive certainty and the ability to maintain practice are based on this.
Aah! Isn't this the time when bodhisattvas practice deep perfection of wisdom? Those with an eye on their foreheads can silently comprehend.

138: On the Lookout

"When outside entanglements stop, the inner mind has no huffing and puffing. When your mind is like a wall, you can enter the Path." Isn't this the model drawn by the First Patriarch at Shaolin? Complete comprehension ever knowing: words cannot reach it. Isn't this the Second Patriarch popping out of the mold?

These days, with minds rent with discontent and mouths babbling on, with one or two teeth like iron spikes, [phony Buddhists] take this mold and with one bite shatter it into a hundred fragments.

Are you the people who can realize the benevolence [of the enlightened teachers] and repay it? I'm on the lookout waiting for such people.

139: What is Buddha?

A monk asked, "What is buddha?" The great teacher Mazu said, "Mind is buddha." Mazu's teacher Huairang of Nanyue heard of this later and said, "Mazu is not there yet. Five more years."

When later on Mazu said, "Not mind, not buddha," Huairang said, "Mazu is still not there. Another five years."

When Mazu said, "It is not mind, not buddha, not things," Huairang said, "He has penetrated through."

Later there was a monk who brought this up to Damei. Damei said, "This old guy will never stop spoiling the sons and daughters of other people's families. For you it's 'not mind, not buddha'. For me it's just 'mind is buddha'."

Stone River commented: "Mazu not only spoiled other people's sons and daughters, he also brought later generations of descendants into error. Where did he go wrong? 'When the whale has drunk the ocean water dry, it reveals the coral branches.'"

NOTES

"When the whale . . . " When the practitioner has exhausted the mind of conditioned perceptions, the mind of delusion, what is revealed is not a blank void, but the totality of reality with its own inherent pattern ("the coral branches").

140: The True Person Without Position

Everyday the eternal pure wind
Thunder runs and lightning rolls
The true person without position
Just puts through a single line

Quick! You must set your eyes on the Immortal
Do not look at the fan in the Immortal's hand

NOTES

"The true person without position" The great Zen teacher Linji said, "Each and everyone of you has a true person without position who is constantly going in and out through the gates of the six senses."

"The fan in the Immortal's hand" the phenomenal world when it veils the underlying absolute reality ("the Immortal").

141: The Bridge

At a ceremony to lay to rest the souls of the dead requested by a patron, Stone River said:

"A monk asked Fuyan, 'A hundred years from now [after I'm dead], what shall I use as a bridge?' Fuyan pointed to his heart and said, 'Take this as the bridge.' The monk pointed to his heart too and said, 'What is this?' Fuyan said, 'Just practice good things. Do not ask about the journey ahead.'

Stone River said in verse:

Brought along for a hundred years to be a bridge
Directly pointing to the field of the heart: this is the site of
    enlightenment
The 84,000 dharmas of peace and bliss
Can be taken up right here

Then Stone River pointed to his breast.